6. Enter your class ID code to join a class.

IF YOU HAVE A CLASS CODE FROM YOUR TEACHER

a. Enter your class code and click [Next]

b. Once you have joined a class, you will be able to u the Discussion Board and Email tools.

c. To enter this code later, choose **Join a Class**.

IF YOU DO NOT HAVE A CLASS CODE

a. If you do not have a class ID code, click [Skip]

b. You do not need a class ID code to use *iQ Online*.

c. To enter this code later, choose **Join a Class**.

7. Review registration information and click Log In. Then choose your book. Click **Activities** to begin using *iQ Online*.

IMPORTANT

- After you register, the next time you want to use *iQ Online*, go to www.iQOnlinePractice.com and log in with your email address and password.
- The online content can be used for 12 months from the date you register.
- For help, please contact customer service: eltsupport@oup.com.

WHAT IS iQ ONLINE ?

All new activities provide essential skills **practice** and support.

Vocabulary and Grammar **games** immerse you in the language and provide even more practice.

Authentic, engaging **videos** generate new ideas and opinions on the Unit Question.

Go to the Media Center to download or stream all **student book audio**.

Use the **Discussion Board** to discuss the Unit Question and more.

Email encourages communication with your teacher and classmates.

Automatic grading gives immediate feedback and tracks progress.

Progress Reports show what you have mastered and where you still need more practice.

SHAPING learning TOGETHER

We would like to acknowledge the teachers from all over the world who participated in the development process and review of the Q series.

Special thanks to our *Q: Skills for Success* Second Edition Topic Advisory Board

Shaker Ali Al-Mohammad, Buraimi University College, Oman; **Dr. Asmaa A. Ebrahim**, University of Sharjah, U.A.E.; **Rachel Batchilder**, College of the North Atlantic, Qatar; **Anil Bayir**, Izmir University, Turkey; **Flora Mcvay Bozkurt**, Maltepe University, Turkey; **Paul Bradley**, University of the Thai Chamber of Commerce Bangkok, Thailand; **Joan Birrell-Bertrand**, University of Manitoba, MB, Canada; **Karen E. Caldwell**, Zayed University, U.A.E.; **Nicole Hammond Carrasquel**, University of Central Florida, FL, U.S.; **Kevin Countryman**, Seneca College of Applied Arts & Technology, ON, Canada; **Julie Crocker**, Arcadia University, NS, Canada; **Marc L. Cummings**, Jefferson Community and Technical College, KY, U.S.; **Rachel DeSanto**, Hillsborough Community College Dale Mabry Campus, FL, U.S.; **Nilüfer Ertürkmen**, Ege University, Turkey; **Sue Fine**, Ras Al Khaimah Women's College (HCT), U.A.E.; **Amina Al Hashami**, Nizwa College of Applied Sciences, Oman; **Stephan Johnson**, Nagoya Shoka Daigaku, Japan; **Sean Kim**, Avalon, South Korea; **Gregory King**, Chubu Daigaku, Japan; **Seran Küçük**, Maltepe University, Turkey; **Jonee De Leon**, VUS, Vietnam; **Carol Lowther**, Palomar College, CA, U.S.; **Erin Harris-MacLead**, St. Mary's University, NS, Canada; **Angela Nagy**, Maltepe University, Turkey; **Huynh Thi Ai Nguyen**, Vietnam; **Daniel L. Paller**, Kinjo Gakuin University, Japan; **Jangyo Parsons**, Kookmin University, South Korea; **Laila Al Qadhi**, Kuwait University, Kuwait; **Josh Rosenberger**, English Language Institute University of Montana, MT, U.S.; **Nancy Schoenfeld**, Kuwait University, Kuwait; **Jenay Seymour**, Hongik University, South Korea; **Moon-young Son**, South Korea; **Matthew Taylor**, Kinjo Gakuin Daigaku, Japan; **Burcu Tezcan-Unal**, Zayed University, U.A.E.; **Troy Tucker**, Edison State College-Lee Campus, FL, U.S.; **Kris Vicca**, Feng Chia University, Taichung; **Jisook Woo**, Incheon University, South Korea; **Dunya Yenidunya**, Ege University, Turkey

UNITED STATES **Marcarena Aguilar**, North Harris College, TX; **Rebecca Andrade**, California State University North Ridge, CA; **Lesley Andrews**, Boston University, MA; **Deborah Anholt**, Lewis and Clark College, OR; **Robert Anzelde**, Oakton Community College, IL; **Arlys Arnold**, University of Minnesota, MN; **Marcia Arthur**, Renton Technical College, WA; **Renee Ashmeade**, Passaic County Community College, NJ; **Anne Bachmann**, Clackamas Community College, OR; **Lida Baker**, UCLA, CA; **Ron Balsamo**, Santa Rosa Junior College, CA; **Lori Barkley**, Portland State University, OR; **Eileen Barlow**, SUNY Albany, NY; **Sue Bartch**, Cuyahoga Community College, OH; **Lora Bates**, Oakton High School, VA; **Barbara Batra**, Nassau County Community College, NY; **Nancy Baum**, University of Texas at Arlington, TX; **Rebecca Beck**, Irvine Valley College, CA; **Linda Berendsen**, Oakton Community College, IL; **Jennifer Binckes Lee**, Howard Community College, MD; **Grace Bishop**, Houston Community College, TX; **Jean W. Bodman**, Union County College, NJ; **Virginia Bouchard**, George Mason University, VA; **Kimberley Briesch Sumner**, University of Southern California, CA; **Kevin Brown**, University of California, Irvine, CA; **Laura Brown**, Glendale Community College, CA; **Britta Burton**, Mission College, CA; **Allison L. Callahan**, Harold Washington College, IL; **Gabriela Cambiasso**, Harold Washington College, IL; **Jackie Campbell**, Capistrano Unified School District, CA; **Adele C. Camus**, George Mason University, VA; **Laura Chason**, Savannah College, GA; **Kerry Linder Catana**, Language Studies International, NY; **An Cheng**, Oklahoma State University, OK; **Carole Collins**, North Hampton Community College, PA; **Betty R. Compton**, Intercultural Communications College, HI; **Pamela Couch**, Boston University, MA; **Fernanda Crowe**, Intrax International Institute, CA; **Vicki Curtis**, Santa Cruz, CA; **Margo Czinski**, Washtenaw Community College, MI; **David Dahnke**, Lone Star College, TX; **Gillian M. Dale**, CA; **L. Dalgish**, Concordia College, MN; **Christopher Davis**, John Jay College, NY; **Sherry Davis**, Irvine University, CA; **Natalia de Cuba**, Nassau County Community College, NY; **Sonia Delgadillo**, Sierra College, CA; **Esmeralda Diriye**, Cypress College & Cal Poly, CA; **Marta O. Dmytrenko-Ahrabian**, Wayne State University, MI; **Javier Dominguez**, Central High School, SC; **Jo Ellen Downey-Greer**, Lansing Community College, MI; **Jennifer Duclos**, Boston University, MA; **Yvonne Duncan**, City College of San Francisco, CA; **Paul Dydman**, USC Language Academy, CA; **Anna Eddy**, University of Michigan-Flint, MI; **Zohan El-Gamal**, Glendale Community College, CA; **Jennie Farnell**, University of Connecticut, CT; **Susan Fedors**, Howard Community College, MD; **Valerie Fiechter**, Mission College, CA; **Ashley Fifer**, Nassau County Community College, NY; **Matthew Florence**, Intrax International Institute, CA; **Kathleen Flynn**, Glendale College, CA; **Elizabeth Fonsea**, Nassau County Community College, NY; **Eve Fonseca**, St. Louis Community College, MO; **Elizabeth Foss**, Washtenaw Community College, MI; **Duff C. Galda**, Pima Community College, AZ; **Christiane Galvani**, Houston Community College, TX; **Gretchen Gerber**, Howard Community College, MD; **Ray Gonzalez**, Montgomery College, MD; **Janet Goodwin**, University of California, Los Angeles, CA; **Alyona Gorokhova**, Grossmont College, CA; **John Graney**, Santa Fe College, FL; **Kathleen Green**, Central High School, AZ; **Nancy Hamadou**, Pima Community College-West Campus, AZ; **Webb Hamilton**, De Anza College, San Jose City College, CA; **Janet Harclerode**, Santa Monica Community College, CA; **Sandra Hartmann**, Language and Culture Center, TX; **Kathy Haven**, Mission College, CA; **Roberta Hendrick**, Cuyahoga Community College, OH; **Ginny Heringer**, Pasadena City College, CA; **Adam Henricksen**, University of Maryland, MD; **Carolyn Ho**, Lone Star College-CyFair, TX; **Peter Hoffman**, LaGuardia Community College, NY; **Linda Holden**, College of Lake County, IL; **Jana Holt**, Lake Washington Technical College, WA; **Antonio Iccarino**, Boston University, MA; **Gail Ibele**, University of Wisconsin, WI; **Nina Ito**, American Language Institute, CSU Long Beach, CA; **Linda Jensen**, UCLA, CA; **Lisa Jurkowitz**, Pima Community College, CA; **Mandy Kama**, Georgetown University, Washington, DC; **Stephanie Kasuboski**, Cuyahoga Community College, OH; **Chigusa Katoku**, Mission College, CA; **Sandra Kawamura**, Sacramento City College, CA; **Gail Kellersberger**, University of Houston-Downtown, TX; **Jane Kelly**, Durham Technical Community College, NC; **Maryanne Kildare**, Nassau County Community College, NY; **Julie Park Kim**, George Mason University, VA; **Kindra Kinyon**, Los Angeles Trade-Technical College, CA; **Matt Kline**, El Camino College, CA; **Lisa Kovacs-Morgan**, University of California, San Diego, CA; **Claudia Kupiec**, DePaul University, IL; **Renee La Rue**, Lone Star College-Montgomery, TX; **Janet Langon**, Glendale College, CA; **Lawrence Lawson**, Palomar College, CA; **Rachele Lawton**, The Community College of Baltimore County, MD; **Alice Lee**, Richland College, TX; **Esther S. Lee**, CSUF & Mt. SAC, CA; **Cherie Lenz-Hackett**, University of Washington, WA; **Joy Leventhal**, Cuyahoga Community College, OH; **Alice Lin**, UCI Extension, CA; **Monica Lopez**, Cerritos College, CA; **Dustin Lovell**, FLS International Marymount College, CA; **Carol Lowther**, Palomar College, CA; **Candace Lynch-Thompson**, North Orange County Community College District, CA; **Thi Thi Ma**, City College of San Francisco, CA; **Steve Mac Isaac**, USC Long Academy, CA; **Denise Maduli-Williams**, City College of San Francisco, CA; **Eileen Mahoney**, Camelback High School, AZ; **Naomi Mardock**, MCC-Omaha, NE; **Brigitte Maronde**, Harold Washington College, IL; **Marilyn Marquis**, Laposita College CA; **Doris Martin**, Glendale Community College; Pasadena City College, CA; **Keith Maurice**, University of Texas at Arlington, TX; **Nancy Mayer**, University of Missouri-St. Louis, MO; **Aziah McNamara**, Kansas State University, KS; **Billie McQuillan**, Education Heights, MN; **Karen Merritt**, Glendale Union High School District, AZ; **Holly Milkowart**, Johnson County Community College, KS; **Eric Moyer**, Intrax International Institute, CA; **Gino Muzzatti**, Santa Rosa Junior College, CA; **Sandra Navarro**, Glendale Community College, CA; **Than Nyeinkhin**, ELAC, PCC, CA; **William Nedrow**, Triton College, IL; **Eric Nelson**, University of Minnesota, MN; **Than Nyeinkhin**, ELAC, PCC, CA; **Fernanda Ortiz**, Center for English as a Second Language at the University of Arizona, AZ; **Rhony Ory**, Ygnacio Valley High School, CA; **Paul Parent**, Montgomery College, MD; **Dr. Sumeeta Patnaik**, Marshall University, WV; **Oscar Pedroso**, Miami Dade College, FL; **Robin Persiani**, Sierra College, CA; **Patricia Prenz-Belkin**, Hostos Community College, NY; **Suzanne Powell**, University of Louisville, KY; **Jim Ranalli**, Iowa State University, IA; **Toni R. Randall**, Santa Monica College, CA; **Vidya Rangachari**, Mission College, CA; **Elizabeth Rasmussen**, Northern Virginia Community College, VA; **Lara Ravitch**, Truman College, IL;

ii

Industry, Vietnam; **Do Thi Thanh Nhan**, Hanoi University, Vietnam; **Dale Kazuo Nishi**, Aoyama English Conversation School, Japan; **Huynh Thi Ai Nguyen**, Vietnam; **Dongshin Oh**, YBM PLS, South Korea; **Keiko Okada**, Dokkyo Daigaku, Japan; **Louise Ohashi**, Shukutoku University, Japan; **Yongjun Park**, Sangji University, South Korea; **Donald Patnaude**, Ajarn Donald's English Language Services, Thailand; **Virginia Peng**, Ritsumeikan University, Japan; **Suangkanok Piboonthamnont**, Rajamangala University of Technology, Thailand; **Simon Pitcher**, Business English Teaching Services, Japan; **John C. Probert**, New Education Worldwide, Thailand; **Do Thi Hoa Quyen**, Ton Duc Thang University, Vietnam; **John P. Racine**, Dokkyo University, Japan; **Kevin Ramsden**, Kyoto University of Foreign Studies, Japan; **Luis Rappaport**, Cung Thieu Nha Ha Noi, Vietnam; **Lisa Reshad**, Konan Daigaku Hyogo, Japan; **Peter Riley**, Taisho University, Japan; **Thomas N. Robb**, Kyoto Sangyo University, Japan; **Rory Rosszell**, Meiji Daigaku, Japan; **Maria Feti Rosyani**, Universitas Kristen Indonesia, Indonesia; **Greg Rouault**, Konan University, Japan; **Chris Ruddenklau**, Kindai University, Japan; **Hans-Gustav Schwartz**, Thailand; **Mary-Jane Scott**, Soongsil University, South Korea; **Dara Sheahan**, Seoul National University, South Korea; **James Sherlock**, A.P.W. Angthong, Thailand; **Prof. Shieh**, Minghsin University of Science & Technology, Xinfeng; **Yuko Shimizu**, Ritsumeikan University, Japan; **Suzila Mohd Shukor**, Universiti Sains Malaysia, Malaysia; **Stephen E. Smith**, Mahidol University, Thailand; **Moon-young Son**, South Korea; **Seunghee Son**, Anyang University, South Korea; **Mi-young Song**, Kyungwon University, South Korea; **Lisa Sood**, VUS, BIS, Vietnam; **Jason Stewart**, Taejon International Language School, South Korea; **Brian A. Stokes**, Korea University, South Korea; **Mulder Su**, Shih-Chien University, Kaohsiung; **Yoomi Suh**, English Plus, South Korea; **Yun-Fang Sun**, Wenzao Ursuline College of Languages, Kaohsiung; **Richard Swingle**, Kansai Gaidai University, Japan; **Sanford Taborn**, Kinjo Gakuin Daigaku, Japan; **Mamoru Takahashi**, Akita Prefectural University, Japan; **Tran Hoang Tan**, School of International Training, Vietnam; **Takako Tanaka**, Doshisha University, Japan; **Jeffrey Taschner**, American University Alumni Language Center, Thailand; **Matthew Taylor**, Kinjo Gakuin Daigaku, Japan; **Michael Taylor**, International Pioneers School, Thailand; **Kampanart Thammaphati**, Wattana Wittaya Academy, Thailand; **Tran Duong The**, Sao Mai Language Center, Vietnam; **Tran Dinh Tho**, Duc Tri Secondary School, Vietnam; **Huynh Thi Anh Thu**, Nhatrang College of Culture Arts and Tourism, Vietnam; **Peter Timmins**, Peter's English School, Japan; **Fumie Togano**, Hosei Daini High School, Japan; **F. Sigmund Topor**, Keio University Language School, Japan; **Tu Trieu**, Rise VN, Vietnam; **Yen-Cheng Tseng**, Chang-Jung Christian University, Tainan; **Pei-Hsuan Tu**, National Cheng Kung University, Tainan City; **Hajime Uematsu**, Hirosaki University, Japan; **Rachel Um**, Mok-dong Oedae English School, South Korea; **David Underhill**, EEExpress, Japan; **Ben Underwood**, Kugenuma High School, Japan; **Siriluck Usaha**, Sripatum University, Thailand; **Tyas Budi Utami**, Indonesia; **Nguyen Thi Van**, Far East International School, Vietnam; **Stephan Van Eycken**, Kosei Gakuen Girls High School, Japan; **Zisa Velasquez**, Taihu International School/Semarang International School, China/Indonesia; **Jeffery Walter**, Sangji University, South Korea; **Bill White**, Kinki University, Japan; **Yohanes De Deo Widyastoko**, Xaverius Senior High School, Indonesia; **Dylan Williams**, SNU, South Korea; **Jisuk Woo**, Ichean University, South Korea; **Greg Chung-Hsien Wu**, Providence University, Taichung; **Xun Xiaoming**, BLCU, China; **Hui-Lien Yeh**, Chai Nan University of Pharmacy and Science, Tainan; **Sittiporn Yodnil**, Huachiew Chalermprakiet University, Thailand; **Shamshul Helmy Zambahari**, Universiti Teknologi Malaysia, Malaysia; **Ming-Yuli**, Chang Jung Christian University, Tainan; **Aimin Fadhlee bin Mahmud Zuhodi**, Kuala Terengganu Science School, Malaysia;

Shirley F. Akis, American Culture Association/Fomara; **Gül Akkoç**, Boğaziçi University; **Seval Akmeşe**, Haliç University; **Ayşenur Akyol**, Ege University; **Ayşe Umut Aribaş**, Beykent University; **Gökhan Asan**, Kapadokya Vocational College; **Hakan Asan**, Kapadokya Vocational College; **Julia Asan**, Kapadokya Vocational College; **Azarvan Atac**, Piri Reis University; **Nur Babat**, Kapadokya Vocational College; **Feyza Balakbabalar**, Kadir Has University; **Gözde Balikçi**, Beykent University; **Deniz Balım**, Haliç University; **Asli Başdoğan**, Kadir Has University; **Ayla Bayram**, Kapadokya Vocational College; **Pinar Bilgiç**, Kadir Has University; **Kenan Bozkurt**, Kapadokya Vocational College; **Yonca Bozkurt**, Ege University; **Frank Carr**, Piri Reis; **Mengü Noyan Çengel**, Ege University; **Elif Doğan**, Ege University; **Natalia Donmez**, 29 Mayis Üniversite; **Nalan Emirsoy**, Kadir Has University; **Ayşe Engin**, Kadir Has University; **Ayhan Gedikbaş**, Ege University; **Gülşah Gençer**, Beykent University; **Seyit Ömer Gök**, Gediz University; **Tuğba Gök**, Gediz University; **İlkay Gökçe**, Ege University; **Zeynep Birinci Guler**, Maltepe University; **Neslihan Güler**, Kadir Has University; **Sircan Gümüş**,

Kadir Has University; **Nesrin Gündoğu**, T.C. Piri Reis University; **Tanju Gurpinar**, Piri Reis University; **Selin Gurturk**, Piri Reis University; **Neslihan Gurutku**, Piri Reis University; **Roger Hewitt**, Maltepe University; **Nilüfer İbrahimoğlu**, Beykent University; **Nevin Kaftelen**, Kadir Has University; **Sultan Kalin**, Kapadokya Vocational College; **Sema Kaplan Karabina**, Anadolu University; **Eray Kara**, Giresun University; **Beylü Karayazgan**, Ege University; **Darren Kelso**, Piri Reis University; **Trudy Kittle**, Kapadokya Vocational College; **Şaziye Konaç**, Kadir Has University; **Güneş Korkmaz**, Kapadokya Vocational College; **Robert Ledbury**, Izmir University of Economics; **Ashley Lucas**, Maltepe University; **Bülent Nedium Uça**, Dogus University; **Murat Nurlu**, Ege University; **Mollie Owens**, Kadir Has University; **Oya Özağaç**, Boğaziçi University; **Funda Özcan**, Ege University; **İlkay Özdemir**, Ege University; **Ülkü Öztürk**, Gediz University; **Cassondra Puls**, Anadolu University; **Yelda Sarikaya**, Cappadocia Vocational College; **Müge Şekercioğlu**, Ege University; **Melis Senol**, Canakkale Onsekiz Mart University, The School of Foreign Languages; **Patricia Sümer**, Kadir Has University; **Rex Surface**, Beykent University; **Mustafa Torun**, Kapadokya Vocational College; **Tansel Üstünloğlu**, Ege University; **Fatih Yücel**, Beykent University; **Şule Yüksel**, Ege University;

Amina Saif Mohammed Al Hashamia, Nizwa College of Applied Sciences, Oman; **Jennifer Baran**, Kuwait University, Kuwait; **Phillip Chappells**, GEMS Modern Academy, U.A.E.; **Sharon Ruth Devaneson**, Ibri College of Technology, Oman; **Hanaa El-Deeb**, Canadian International College, Egypt; **Yvonne Eaton**, Community College of Qatar, Qatar; **Brian Gay**, Sultan Qaboos University, Oman; **Gail Al Hafidh**, Sharjah Women's College (HCT), U.A.E.; **Jonathan Hastings**, American Language Center, Jordan; **Laurie Susan Hilu**, English Language Centre, University of Bahrain, Bahrain; **Abraham Irannezhad**, Mehre Aval, Iran; **Kevin Kempe**, CNA-Q, Qatar; **Jill Newby James**, University of Nizwa; **Mary Kay Klein**, American University of Sharjah, U.A.E.; **Sian Khoury**, Fujairah Women's College (HCT), U.A.E.; **Hussein Dehghan Manshadi**, Farhang Pajooh & Jaam-e-Jam Language School, Iran; **Jessica March**, American University of Sharjah, U.A.E.; **Neil McBeath**, Sultan Qaboos University, Oman; **Sandy McDonagh**, Abu Dhabi Men's College (HCT), U.A.E.; **Rob Miles**, Sharjah Women's College (HCT), U.A.E.; **Michael Kevin Neumann**, Al Ain Men's College (HCT), U.A.E.;

Aldana Aguirre, Argentina; **Claudia Almeida**, Coordenação de Idiomas, Brazil; **Cláudia Arias**, Brazil; **Maria de los Angeles Barba**, FES Acatlan UNAM, Mexico; **Lilia Barrios**, Universidad Autónoma de Tamaulipas, Mexico; **Adán Beristain**, UAEM, Mexico; **Ricardo Böck**, Manoel Ribas, Brazil; **Edson Braga**, CNA, Brazil; **Marli Buttelli**, Mater et Magistra, Brazil; **Alessandra Campos**, Inova Centro de Linguas, Brazil; **Priscila Catta Preta Ribeiro**, Brazil; **Gustavo Cestari**, Access International School, Brazil; **Walter D'Alessandro**, Virginia Language Center, Brazil; **Lilian De Gennaro**, Argentina; **Mônica De Stefani**, Quality Centro de Idiomas, Brazil; **Julio Alejandro Flores**, BUAP, Mexico; **Mirian Freire**, CNA Vila Guilherme, Brazil; **Francisco Garcia**, Colegio Lestonnac de San Angel, Mexico; **Miriam Giovanardi**, Brazil; **Darlene Gonzalez Miy**, ITESM CCV, Mexico; **Maria Laura Grimaldi**, Argentina; **Luz Dary Guzmán**, IMPAHU, Colombia; **Carmen Koppe**, Brazil; **Monica Krutzler**, Brazil; **Marcus Murilo Lacerda**, Seven Idiomas, Brazil; **Nancy Lake**, CEL-LEP, Brazil; **Cris Lazzerini**, Brazil; **Sandra Luna**, Argentina; **Ricardo Luvisan**, Brazil; **Jorge Murilo Menezes**, ACBEU, Brazil; **Monica Navarro**, Instituto Cultural A. C., Mexico; **Joacyr Oliveira**, Faculdades Metropolitanas Unidas and Summit School for Teachers, Brazil; **Ayrton Cesar Oliveira de Araujo**, E&A English Classes, Brazil; **Ana Laura Oriente**, Seven Idiomas, Brazil; **Adelia Peña Clavel**, CELE UNAM, Mexico; **Beatriz Pereira**, Summit School, Brazil; **Miguel Perez**, Instituto Cultural, Mexico; **Cristiane Perone**, Associação Cultura Inglesa, Brazil; **Pamela Claudia Pogré**, Colegio Integral Caballito / Universidad de Flores, Argentina; **Dalva Prates**, Brazil; **Marianne Rampaso**, Iowa Idiomas, Brazil; **Daniela Rutolo**, Instituto Superior Cultural Británico, Argentina; **Maione Sampaio**, Maione Carrijo Consultoria em Inglês Ltda, Brazil; **Elaine Santesso**, TS Escola de Idiomas, Brazil; **Camila Francisco Santos**, UNS Idiomas, Brazil; **Lucia Silva**, Cooplem Idiomas, Brazil; **Maria Adela Sorzio**, Instituto Superior Santa Cecilia, Argentina; **Elcio Souza**, Unibero, Brazil; **Willie Thomas**, Rainbow Idiomas, Brazil; **Sandra Villegas**, Instituto Humberto de Paolis, Argentina; **John Whelan**, La Universidad Nacional Autonoma de Mexico, Mexico

CONTENTS

How to Register for iQ ONLINE i

| **UNIT 5** | **Nutrition** | **102** |

Q: How has science changed the food we eat?
Unit Video: **The Science of Taste** 103
Note-taking Skill: Editing notes after a lecture 105
Listening 1: Food Additives Linked to Hyperactivity in Kids 106
Listening Skill: Understanding bias in a presentation 110
Listening 2: The "Flavr Savr" Tomato 111
Vocabulary Skill: Prefixes and suffixes 116
Grammar: Comparative forms of adjectives and adverbs 118
Pronunciation: Other common intonation patterns 120
Speaking Skill: Expressing interest during a conversation 121
Unit Assignment: Take part in a debate 123

| **UNIT 6** | **Education** | **126** |

Q: Is one road to success better than another?
Note-taking Skill: Comparing and contrasting notes on multiple topics 129
Listening 1: Changing Ways to Climb the Ladder 130
Listening Skill: Listening for contrasting ideas 133
Listening 2: Life Experience Before College 135
Unit Video: Interns in New York 139
Vocabulary Skill: Using the dictionary: formal and informal words 140
Grammar: Simple, compound, and complex sentences 142
Pronunciation: Highlighted words 144
Speaking Skill: Changing the topic 146
Unit Assignment: Reach a group decision 148

| **UNIT 7** | **Anthropology** | **152** |

Q: How can accidental discoveries affect our lives?
Unit Video: **Post-It Note Inventor** 153
Listening 1: The Power of Serendipity 155
Listening Skill: Listening for signal words and phrases 159
Note-taking Skill: Taking notes on details 161
Listening 2: Against All Odds, Twin Girls Reunited 163
Vocabulary Skill: Collocations with prepositions 168
Grammar: Indirect speech 170
Pronunciation: Linked words with vowels 172
Speaking Skill: Using questions to maintain listener interest 173
Unit Assignment: Tell a story 175

| **UNIT 8** | **Social Psychology** | **178** |

Q: Is athletic competition good for children?
Listening 1: Training Chinese Athletes 181
Listening Skill: Listening for causes and effects 186
Note-taking Skill: Taking notes on causes and effects 187
Listening 2: *Until It Hurts* Discusses Youth Sports Obsession 189
Unit Video: Children in Sports 193
Vocabulary Skill: Idioms 193
Grammar: Uses of real conditionals 195
Pronunciation: Thought groups 197
Speaking Skill: Adding to another speaker's comments 198
Unit Assignment: Share opinions about sportsmanship 200

Audio Track List 204
Authors and Consultants 205
Vocabulary List and CEFR Correlation 206–207

UNIT **5**

Nutrition

NOTE TAKING	▶	editing notes after a lecture
LISTENING	▶	understanding bias in a presentation
VOCABULARY	▶	prefixes and suffixes
GRAMMAR	▶	comparative forms of adjectives and adverbs
PRONUNCIATION	▶	other common intonation patterns
SPEAKING	▶	expressing interest during a conversation

UNIT QUESTION

How has science changed the food we eat?

A Discuss these questions with your classmates.

1. Which is more important in the food you choose: flavor, cost, or nutrition? Why?

2. Scientists have developed ways to genetically modify plants. What do you know about genetically modified food?

3. Look at the photo of the fish farm. Would you prefer to eat fish raised on a farm or fish caught from the sea?

◑ B Listen to *The Q Classroom* online. Then answer
these questions.

1. Felix and Marcus state that packaged food is not
healthy. Do you agree? Why or why not?

2. Sophy says that because of science, we can
grow bigger plants and animals. What might be an
advantage to having bigger food?

iQ ONLINE **C** Go online to watch the video about the manufacturing of
flavors. Then check your comprehension.

deliberately *(adv.)* done in a way that
was planned, not by chance

in your face *(phr.)* obvious

palatable *(adj.)* having a pleasant or
acceptable taste

stimulating *(adj.)* making you feel more
excited and healthy

VIDEO VOCABULARY

iQ ONLINE **D** Go to the Online Discussion Board to discuss
the Unit Question with your classmates.

E Think about the food that you usually eat. Then look at the list. Check (✓) the foods that you buy and eat frequently.

What Foods Do You Buy Frequently?

- ☐ bread
- ☐ milk
- ☐ soda
- ☐ meat
- ☐ rice
- ☐ pizza
- ☐ fish

- ☐ breakfast cereal
- ☐ chicken
- ☐ fresh fruit
- ☐ vegetables
- ☐ potato chips
- ☐ chocolate
- ☐ frozen meals

- ☐ canned soup
- ☐ ice cream
- ☐ beans
- ☐ fast food
- ☐ energy drinks
- ☐ other: _____
- ☐ other: _____

F Work in a group. Discuss the selections you made in Activity E. Do you know how those foods are created? Are any of them all natural? Which foods do you think have added chemicals or are genetically modified? Explain. Give reasons for your answers.

In order to remember most of what you hear, it is a good idea to review your notes within 24 hours after a lecture. As you read your notes, **annotate** them (add notes to a text, giving explanations or comments):

1. Underline or highlight key ideas.

2. Cross out information that isn't important.

3. Use the extra space on the paper to add your thoughts and make connections between the lecture and the information in your textbook.

4. Use a dictionary to look up all new key words. Write the definition or translation.

5. Make notes about what you don't understand so you can ask your teacher later.

6. Add a short summary of your notes.

A. Listen to the lecture about food as medicine. Then edit the notes based on the first four annotation tips above. Compare your edits with a partner.

Peking duck

shark liver oil

Zootherapy—using food in place of medicine
1. *China—Peking Duck*
   a. *Famous and delicious*
   b. *Red rice powder on duck skin*
   c. *Lowers cholesterol (?)*
   d. *Fewer Chinese people get heart disease than other countries*
2. *Brazil—Hammerhead shark liver oil*
   a. *Indigenous (native) populations off the coast of Brazil*
   b. *Cure asthma (trouble breathing)*
   c. *Endangered (?)*
   d. *Now, researchers are testing asthma drugs made from oil from nurse & blue sharks*

B. Review the notes again. Write two follow-up questions and a short summary based on the fifth and sixth annotation tips above. Share your summary with a partner.

 C. Go online for more practice editing notes after a lecture.

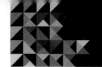

LISTENING

LISTENING 1 | Food Additives Linked to Hyperactivity in Kids

 You are going to listen to a radio report about food chemicals and their effects on children's behavior. As you listen to the report, gather information and ideas about how science has changed the food we eat.

PREVIEW THE LISTENING

A. **PREVIEW** Work with a partner. Why might chemicals in food affect a child's behavior? Give reasons for your answer.

B. **VOCABULARY** Read aloud these words from Listening 1. Check (✓) the ones you know. Use a dictionary to define any new or unknown words. Then discuss with a partner how the words will relate to the unit.

adverse *(adj.)*	**identical** *(adj.)*
artificial *(adj.)* 🔑	**optimal** *(adj.)*
consist of *(phr. v.)* 🔑	**significant** *(adj.)* 🔑
consume *(v.)*	**substantial** *(adj.)* 🔑
controversy *(n.)*	**superfluous** *(adj.)*

🔑 Oxford 3000™ words

 C. Go online to listen and practice your pronunciation.

WORK WITH THE LISTENING

A. **LISTEN AND TAKE NOTES** Listen to the radio report. Complete the student's notes about Professor Stevenson's research.

Professor Stevenson's Study	• Controversy • United Kingdom • _____ children were studied • The additives in this study were _____ and _____

Children	• 2 groups
	    • ____-year-olds
	    • _____-year-olds

What the children received	• _____
	OR _____
	    • Equal to 2 X 50-gram bag of candy
	    • Equal to 4 X 50-gram bag of candy

Results	• Additives can _____ hyperactive behavior in children. • Parents should limit additives in children's food to help _____ hyperactivity. • Not everyone agrees.

B. Edit the notes. Underline or highlight key words and phrases and cross out words that are not important. Also, explain or define new vocabulary and make notes about what you still don't understand.

C. Work with a partner. Use your notes to summarize what Professor Stevenson did in his research project and what his results showed.

D. Listen to the radio report again. Check (✓) the main ideas mentioned in the report.

☐ Artificial additives can make young children hyperactive.

☐ Some of the fruit juice had more food coloring than the rest.

☐ Food coloring significantly affects the behavior of some children.

☐ Preservatives have an important function in food.

☐ Dr. Feingold has written several books.

☐ The study is a source of controversy because some other studies do not have the same results.

☐ Feeding children heavily processed food is not optimal for health.

☐ The study is well designed and important.

E. Read the comments below. Do the speakers agree or disagree with Professor Stevenson's results? Write *A* (agree) or *D* (disagree).

_____ 1. "Professor Stevenson's findings are very interesting. But there are many possible causes of hyperactivity. It is too easy to blame food additives."

_____ 2. "The results of this research are very important. Parents need to be aware of the effects of what their children consume."

_____ 3. "I would like to know how Professor Stevenson defined hyperactivity exactly. How did the observers, the teachers and parents, measure it? Until I understand this, I have doubts about the results."

_____ 4. "Professor Stevenson has confirmed what I have known all along! My son is definitely more hyper after drinking an artificial drink."

_____ 5. "It's too difficult to control the variables in a study like this. It is not possible that Dr. Stevenson could make sure the children consumed only natural food and drinks during his six-week study."

_____ 6. "Simply put, pure food without chemicals is healthier. I am glad science is finally proving this basic fact."

F. VOCABULARY Here are some words from Listening 1. Read the definitions. Then write each bold word next to the correct definition.

1. The plan to build a big road though the neighborhood caused a lot of **controversy**. Many residents disagreed with it.

2. I don't have time to take care of real plants, so I have **artificial** plants in my home. I don't have to worry about watering or feeding them.

3. The results of the study were **significant**, so the scientists wrote about them in a scientific journal.

4. It rained for three days. The **adverse** weather conditions made it impossible for us to enjoy our vacation.

5. My friend's sons are **identical** twins. The boys look so similar that I often mistake one for the other.

6. Teenage boys often **consume** a lot of food because they are growing quickly.

7. The additional information was **superfluous** because I had already made up my mind. I didn't need to hear more about the topic.

8. Researchers have found a **substantial** link between high-cholesterol diets and heart disease. Their research shows the importance of healthy eating.

9. A vegetarian diet may **consist of** mostly vegetables, fruit, grains, and beans. Meat is not part of a vegetarian's diet.

10. Warm, sunny weather is **optimal** for spending a day at the beach.

a. _____ (*adj.*) making something difficult

b. _____ (*adj.*) not natural; made by people

c. _____ (*phr. v.*) to be made up of

d. _____ (*v.*) to eat or drink something

e. _____ (*adj.*) exactly the same as something else

f. _____ (*adj.*) the best possible

g. _____ (*n.*) public discussion and disagreement

h. _____ (*adj.*) great or important

i. _____ (*adj.*) very large or important amount

j. _____ (*adj.*) more than what you need or want

 G. Go online for more practice with the vocabulary.

 ## SAY WHAT YOU THINK

Discuss the questions in a group.

1. How concerned are you about the additives in your food? Do you avoid food that contains additives?

2. Preservatives are added to food to keep it fresh for a longer period of time. Do you think the advantages outweigh the disadvantages? Explain.

3. Should there be stricter rules about the food additives in foods children commonly consume? Why or why not?

Bias is a strong feeling for or against something. Understanding the bias in a presentation is important. Speakers may express biases even when they're trying to sound objective. In Listening 1, the speaker presents research both for and against a link between food additives and hyperactivity, but the speaker's bias appears to be against food additives.

There are several clues to help you understand the bias of a presentation.

Title: Listening 1 is "Food Additives Linked to Hyperactivity in Kids." This is a negative idea, and it sounds very definite. This probably means the speaker agrees with the research in the report. A different title such as "Some Researchers Believe Food Additives May Affect Hyperactivity" does not show such a strong bias.

Introduction: Pay attention to how a speaker introduces a topic. For example, if a speaker starts with, *I'm going to talk about the negative effects of food additives on children's behavior*, that statement alone tells you the speaker's bias.

Imbalance: Reports with a bias usually report on both sides of the issue, but the information is not balanced well. In Listening 1, most of the report is about the research results that show a link between additives and hyperactivity, and only a small part of the report is about research that doesn't show any link.

Information source: Consider who is providing the information. For example, suppose a company that sells chocolate presents research that shows eating chocolate is good for you. Knowing the company sells chocolate can help you decide how much to trust the information.

A. Listen to the short report. Then answer the questions.

1. Check (✓) the clues you hear that tell you the bias.
   - ☐ Title
   - ☐ Introduction
   - ☐ Imbalance
   - ☐ Information source

2. Is the speaker against or in favor of organic food?

   _____

B. Listen to excerpts from four news reports. What bias is being shown in each report? Circle the correct answers.

Excerpt 1

a. Some scientists believe there are many causes of obesity.

b. Some scientists believe fast food is the main cause of obesity.

Excerpt 2

a. Drinking soda may cause heart disease.

b. Drinking soda is part of a healthy lifestyle.

Excerpt 3

a. Drinking too much tea can be harmful.

b. Drinking tea is an old tradition.

Excerpt 4

a. Food labels can help us make good choices.

b. Food labels can be difficult to believe.

 C. Go online for more practice understanding bias in a presentation.

LISTENING 2 | The "Flavr Savr" Tomato

 You are going to listen to a news report about a genetically engineered, or altered, tomato called the "Flavr Savr" tomato. Scientists created this tomato to give it particular traits. As you listen to the report, gather information and ideas about how science has changed the food we eat.

PREVIEW THE LISTENING

A. **PREVIEW** Do you think altering the genes of plants is a good thing? Why or why not? Discuss with a partner.

B. **VOCABULARY** Read aloud these words from Listening 2. Check (✓) the ones you know. Use a dictionary to define any new or unknown words. Then discuss with a partner how the words will relate to the unit.

alter *(v.)* 🔑	consumer *(n.)* 🔑	ethics *(n.)*	reaction *(n.)* 🔑
commodity *(n.)*	debate *(n.)* 🔑	hurdle *(n.)*	trait *(n.)*
compound *(v.)*	disturbing *(adj.)* 🔑	modification *(n.)*	ultimate *(adj.)* 🔑

🔑 Oxford 3000™ words

 C. Go online to listen and practice your pronunciation.

WORK WITH THE LISTENING

A. **LISTEN AND TAKE NOTES** Listen to the news report. Complete the notes on the speakers and their comments.

Speaker	Job/Role	Comments
Kensington Fruit Market shoppers	customers	• wouldn't buy GMO food • wants to know what goes into the food and _____ • doesn't want to tamper with _____ • people are _____

Nina Winham	news reporter	• genetic engineering = _____
		
		• _____:
		  – insulin
		  – human growth hormone
		
		• GMO food expected to _____

Robert Strong	professor who studies the ethics of biotechnology	• People think modern life is _____. • unnatural = _____
Steven Burke	vice president of North Carolina Biotechnology Center	• with food biotechnology, people interested in the _____ and the _____—b/c we eat it
Susan Harlander	director of research at Land o' Lakes Dairies	• need to show benefits of biotechnology (e.g., _____) • work in lab is continuation of science of farming (e.g., _____) • more _____ in lab than farm
Linda Arugio	vendor at Kensington Fruit Market	• not different from other hybrid products (e.g., _____) • get used to _____

B. Compare your notes with a partner. Whose comments and opinions do you agree with? Why? Have any of the speakers changed the way you think about genetically modified food?

C. Listen to the news report again. Circle the correct answers.

1. In general, the consumers in the news report ____.
   a. didn't like the idea of biotechnology
   b. didn't have strong feelings about biotechnology
   c. didn't understand biotechnology

2. According to the news report, ____.
   a. consumers will not buy genetically altered food
   b. consumers are very excited about genetically altered food
   c. consumers are not sure if genetically altered food is safe

3. According to the report, genetically modified foods will probably ____.
   a. cost less than naturally grown foods
   b. become popular as people get used to them
   c. be banned by governments

4. In general, the report was ____.
   a. in favor of genetically modified foods
   b. against genetically modified foods
   c. not biased about genetically modified foods

D. Read the statements. Write *T* (true) or *F* (false). Then correct the false statements.

____ 1. The "Flavr Savr" tomato is supposed to stay riper longer than an ordinary tomato.

_____

____ 2. Science has influenced farming for a long time.

_____

____ 3. Genetic modification is only used for food.

_____

____ 4. Many people like watermelon with no seeds. This shows people are willing to eat some genetically altered food.

_____

____ 5. The biggest hurdle to getting people to buy genetically modified food may be the cost.

_____

E. Read the comments below. Which of the speakers from the radio report would be most likely to say them? Match the speaker to the comment.

_____ 1. Nina Winham (news reporter)

a. People don't realize that food biotechnology has advantages, too. Customers can enjoy food that tastes better; farmers don't have to focus on breeding or selection; and producers can ship food over long distances without it rotting.

_____ 2. Kensington Fruit Market shoppers

b. We are excited about the new products we are developing. For instance, we are working on creating a kind of new rice that can grow even in very dry conditions. This will feed people all over the world.

_____ 3. Robert Strong (professor who studies the ethics of biotechnology)

c. Customers here buy a lot of tofu because they think it's healthy, but many of them don't realize that it is probably made from genetically modified soybeans.

_____ 4. Steven Burke (vice president of North Carolina Biotechnology Center)

d. As part of my research, we have also discovered that, unsurprisingly, profit is pushing companies toward more and more genetic engineering. They often want to make money. They don't always consider the impact on consumers.

_____ 5. Susan Harlander (director of research at Land o' Lakes Dairies)

e. In our time at the market, we interviewed many customers and almost all reported feeling quite concerned about genetically modifying food.

_____ 6. Linda Arugio (vendor at Kensington Fruit Market)

f. I think companies must put labels on the genetically modified food so we know what we are buying and can make an informed choice.

Vocabulary Skill Review

In Unit 4, you learned about word forms. Try to find different word forms for the following vocabulary words in Activity F: _consumer, disturbing, modification, ethics, reaction._ Use a dictionary to help you.

F. **VOCABULARY** Here are some words from Listening 2. Complete each sentence with the correct word.

alter (v.)	consumer (n.)	ethics (n.)	reaction (n.)
commodity (n.)	debate (n.)	hurdle (n.)	trait (n.)
compound (v.)	disturbing (adj.)	modification (n.)	ultimate (adj.)

1. I don't eat enough vegetables. To _____ the problem, my

grocery store does not have much fresh produce.

2. Getting people to eat newly created foods is a _____ that many companies must deal with. They work hard to make their products marketable.

3. I find it very _____ that people eat so much processed food. How can they eat that stuff instead of fruits and vegetables?

4. Advertisers try to catch the interest of any _____ who will want to buy their products.

5. When they said the newly created carrots were bright red, my first _____ was to say I didn't believe it.

6. We need to _____ our diet. I want to reduce the amount of processed food we eat.

7. Some people wanted the new factory in their town and some didn't. The _____ over building the new factory went on for years.

8. This plant has an important _____ that makes it able to survive in a dry area.

9. Milk is a valuable _____. When cows can't produce enough, the price of milk goes up quickly.

10. I think a bowl of ice cream with hot fudge sauce is the _____ dessert. Nothing could be better than that!

11. I question the _____ of creating "super foods." I'm not sure I agree that genetic engineering is always good.

12. This corn is very similar to normal corn, but scientists made a small _____ to its genes that makes it resist disease.

a corn field

G. Go online for more practice with the vocabulary.

H. Go online to listen to *Superfoods* and check your comprehension.

SAY WHAT YOU THINK

A. Discuss the questions in a group.

1. Some genetically altered plants need less water to grow, are resistant to insects, or are more nutritious. Farmers may be able to feed more people by growing genetically modified crops. Do the benefits of growing genetically modified crops outweigh possible risks? Give reasons for your answer.

2. In some countries, genetically altered foods must have a label explaining that they are altered. Is this law a good idea? Why or why not?

B. Think about the unit video, Listening 1, and Listening 2 as you discuss the questions.

Do you know if any foods you eat have been genetically modified? Do you know which foods contain additives? How can you find out? How will this information affect what you buy?

Vocabulary Skill | Prefixes and suffixes

Prefixes

Adding a **prefix** to the beginning of a word changes the meaning of the word. Understanding a prefix can help you identify the meaning of a word. Here are some prefixes you heard in this unit.

Prefix	Meaning	Example
dis-	opposite of	disorders
under-	less than enough	underdeveloped
re-	again	rebound
un-	not	uneasy

Suffixes

Adding a suffix to the end of a word often changes the part of speech. For example, adding *-ly* to the adjective *wide* changes the word to the adverb *widely*. Here are some examples of common suffixes used in Listening 2.

Suffix	Meaning	Example
-al, -ic	(*adj.*) about, connected with	chemical, genetic
-(at)ion	(*n.*) a state or process	reaction
-ist	(*n.*) a person who does	scientist
-less	(*adj.*) not having something	seedless
-(al)ly	(*adv.*) in a particular way	genetically
-ness	(*n.*) a quality	freshness

A. Write the meaning of each word. Look at the prefixes in the chart on page 116 to help you.

1. disapprove _____

2. redo _____

3. unfair _____

4. underfeed _____

5. untie _____

6. dislike _____

B. Look at the words and phrases below. Write the correct form of the word. Use the suffixes in the chart above to help you.

Tip for Success

Many words drop letters before a suffix is added. Look in the dictionary to see if there are spelling changes when adding suffixes to a word.

1. science (*n.* person) _____scientist_____

2. origin (*adv.*) _____

3. unique (*n.* quality) _____

4. no weight (*adj.*) _____

5. about a topic (*adj.*) _____

6. relate (*n.*) _____

C. Choose five words from Activities A and B. Write a sentence for each word. Then take turns reading your sentences to a partner.

 D. Go online for more practice with prefixes and suffixes.

SPEAKING

 **UNIT OBJECTIVE** ▶▶▶▶ At the end of this unit, you are going to participate in a debate on food science, stating and supporting your opinions about food modification. During the debate, you will need to be able to use comparative forms of adjectives and adverbs and express interest in a conversation.

Grammar | Comparative forms of adjectives and adverbs

Comparative forms of adjectives and adverbs compare two things or actions. The rules for making comparatives are similar for both adjectives and adverbs.

Condition	Rule	Example
one-syllable adjectives	add -er	older
one-syllable adverbs		faster
one-syllable adjectives ending in -e	add -r	nicer
two-syllable adjectives ending in -y	change the y to i and add -er	healthier
most other adjectives	use more or less before the word	more interesting
all other adverbs		less naturally

Some adjectives take either –er or more.

narrow	→	narrower, more narrow
simple	→	simpler, more simple
quiet	→	quieter, more quiet
gentle	→	gentler, more gentle
handsome	→	handsomer, more handsome

Some adjectives and adverbs are irregular. This means the comparative adjective and adverb forms are not based on the base forms.

good	→	better	badly	→	worse
well	→	better	far	→	farther / further
bad	→	worse	little	→	less

To compare things or actions, use the word *than* after the comparative adjective or adverb.

Vegetables are healthier **than** junk food.
Many people are concerned about eating more healthfully **than** they were in the past.

A. Write the comparative forms of the adjectives and adverbs. Then work with a partner. Take turns saying sentences using these comparative forms.

1. flavorful _____

2. uneasy _____

3. high _____

4. tasty _____

5. widely _____

6. unnatural _____

7. acceptable _____

8. bad _____

9. loyal _____

10. expensive _____

B. Work with a partner. Take turns asking and answering comparative questions.

Example: peach / flavorful / preserved / fresh

> *A: Which kind of peach do you think is more flavorful, preserved or fresh?*
> *B: I think fresh peaches are more flavorful than preserved peaches.*

1. juice / sweet / pineapple / orange

2. ice cream / tasty / chocolate / strawberry

3. TV show / disturbing / the news / reality TV

4. drink / widely enjoyed / tea / coffee

5. food / expensive / organic / genetically engineered

C. Go online for more practice with comparative forms of adjectives and adverbs.

D. Go online for the grammar expansion.

<table>
<tr><td>Pronunciation</td><td>Other common intonation patterns</td></tr>
</table>

Intonation is an important part of communicating your ideas. There are common intonation patterns for specific conversational actions. Make sure you are using the correct pattern to help express your meaning.

To ask for clarification, use a rising intonation.

> This tomato is genetically altered?
> **Meaning:** I am not sure I heard you, or I am not sure I understand you.

To express surprise, use a rising intonation.

> You eat five sandwiches a day?
> **Meaning:** I am surprised by this information.

To list items, use a rising intonation for each item on the list. For the last item, use a rising/falling intonation.

> I ate eggs, toast, and cereal.
> **Meaning:** I ate these three things.

For *yes/no* questions, use a rising intonation.

> Would you like coffee?
> **Meaning:** You can say *yes* or *no* to my question.

To offer a choice between two things, use a rising/falling intonation.

> Would you like coffee or iced tea?
> **Meaning:** Which would you prefer?

A. Listen to the sentences. Draw intonation arrows over each one. Then practice saying the sentences with a partner.

1. What? You've never eaten a tomato?

2. Do you prefer water or juice?

3. My favorite foods are rice, yams, and pizza.

4. What did you say? You don't like ice cream?

5. Are you hungry? Do you want some bread and cheese?

Tip for Success

When you listen to the radio, focus on the speakers' intonation. Pay attention to how they use their voices to express ideas and emotions.

B. Work with a partner. Take turns asking and answering the questions. Ask follow-up questions if needed. Focus on using the correct intonation.

1. What are your favorite foods?

2. What are three foods you would never try?

3. Who usually cooks at your house?

C. Go online for more practice with other common intonation patterns.

Speaking Skill Expressing interest during a conversation

Expressing interest during a conversation shows the speaker you are paying attention. There are several ways to express interest in the speaker's ideas. In addition to leaning forward and making eye contact, you can use special words and phrases to show you are interested.

Encouraging words: Yeah. / Wow! / Mm-hmm. / Cool!
Comments: How interesting! / That's amazing!
Emphasis questions: Really?
Repeating words: Speaker: I went to Paris. You: Oh, Paris!

It is not necessary to wait until the speaker has finished talking to use these words and phrases. You can use them throughout the conversation, whenever the speaker completes a thought.

A. Listen to the conversation between two students who are eating lunch. Fill in the blanks with the words in the box. Then practice the conversation with a partner.

mm-hmm	that's interesting	wow
really	every day	yeah

Faisal: Hey, Marc. Is this seat free? Do you mind if I sit here?

Marc: Not at all. How are you doing?

Faisal: I'm absolutely starving!

Marc: _____? Why?
                    1

Faisal: I went to the gym this morning before school, and by 11:00, my stomach was growling in class.

Marc: _____, that had to be embarrassing.
                    2

Faisal: Definitely. So, what did you get for lunch?

Marc: Well, they're serving French onion soup today, so I got some of that. It's not bad, but not like home!

Faisal: _____! French food is famous around the world, but
                     3
I've never had it.

Marc: Well, I am from Provence, in the south of France. People take food very seriously there.

Faisal: _____.
                    4

Marc: People buy fresh fruit and vegetables from the market every day.

Faisal: _____?
                    5

Marc: Yeah, and the cheese is amazing! It tastes nothing like what we buy in the grocery stores here.

Faisal: _____. I feel that way about Saudi Arabian food here,
                    6
too. It's not quite the same.

B. Work in a group to answer the questions. As you listen, use different ways to express interest and show you are paying attention.

1. What food or drink would you recommend to someone who has a cold? Are there any traditional remedies you use in your family?

2. Which meal is the most important of the day to you? Why?

3. Can you cook? If so, what is a dish that you make particularly well? How do you make it?

 C. Go online for more practice expressing interest during a conversation.

UNIT
OBJECTIVE ▶▶▶▶

In this assignment, you are going to present your opinions in a debate on food science. As you prepare your opinions, think about the Unit Question, "How has science changed the food we eat?" Use information from Listening 1, Listening 2, the unit video, and your work in this unit to support your opinions. Refer to the Self-Assessment checklist on page 124.

CONSIDER THE IDEAS

Critical Thinking (Tip)

In the Consider the Ideas discussion, you have to give reasons to **support** your opinion. When you support your opinion, you put ideas together from different sources. This allows you to use information in new ways.

Work in a group. Discuss the photos below. What do you think the advantages and disadvantages of each of these modifications are? Give reasons to support your opinion.

Raspberries preserved by radiation, a type of energy that can cause illness in large amounts

Raspberries that have not been preserved by radiation

A chicken that eats non-chemically treated food

A chicken that eats food that has been treated with artificial chemicals to make it grow much larger than normal

PREPARE AND SPEAK

A. GATHER IDEAS Think about the opinions you shared in the Consider the Ideas activity. Which ideas did you find most convincing? Make a short list of the three most convincing opinions on this issue.

B. ORGANIZE IDEAS Put the reasons from your list into the chart. Add details and examples to support the reasons.

Reasons	Details and examples
1.	
2.	
3.	

C. SPEAK Work with a partner who has different opinions on this issue. Take turns presenting your opinions and the reasons that support them. Show interest in your partner's opinions and ask questions to get more information. Refer to the Self-Assessment checklist before you begin.

 Go online for your alternate Unit Assignment.

CHECK AND REFLECT

A. CHECK Think about the Unit Assignment as you complete the Self-Assessment checklist.

SELF-ASSESSMENT		
Yes	No	
☐	☐	I was able to speak easily about the topic.
☐	☐	My partner, group, and class understood me.
☐	☐	I used comparative forms of adjectives and adverbs.
☐	☐	I used vocabulary from the unit.
☐	☐	I expressed interest during the conversation.
☐	☐	I used common intonation patterns correctly.

B. **REFLECT** **Go to the Online Discussion Board to discuss these questions.**

1. What is something new you learned in this unit?

2. Look back at the Unit Question—How has science changed the food we eat? Is your answer different now than when you started this unit? If yes, how is it different? Why?

TRACK YOUR SUCCESS

Circle the words you have learned in this unit.

Nouns	Verbs	Adjectives
commodity **AWL**	alter 🔑 **AWL**	adverse
consumer 🔑 **AWL**	compound **AWL**	artificial 🔑
controversy **AWL**	consume **AWL**	disturbing 🔑
debate 🔑 **AWL**		identical **AWL**
ethics **AWL**	**Phrasal verb**	optimal
hurdle	consist of 🔑 **AWL**	significant 🔑 **AWL**
modification **AWL**		substantial 🔑
reaction 🔑 **AWL**		superfluous
trait		ultimate 🔑 **AWL**

🔑 Oxford 3000™ words
AWL Academic Word List

Check (✓) the skills you learned. If you need more work on a skill, refer to the page(s) in parentheses.

NOTE TAKING ■	I can edit my notes after a lecture. (p. 105)
LISTENING ■	I can understand bias in a presentation. (p. 110)
VOCABULARY ■	I can recognize and use prefixes and suffixes. (pp. 116–117)
GRAMMAR ■	I can use comparative forms of adjectives and adverbs. (p. 118)
PRONUNCIATION ■	I can use common intonation patterns. (p. 120)
SPEAKING ■	I can express interest during a conversation. (p. 121)
UNIT OBJECTIVE ▶▶▶▶ ■	I can gather information and ideas to participate in a debate on food science.

NOTE TAKING	▶	comparing and contrasting notes on multiple topics
LISTENING	▶	listening for contrasting ideas
VOCABULARY	▶	using the dictionary: formal and informal words
GRAMMAR	▶	simple, compound, and complex sentences
PRONUNCIATION	▶	highlighted words
SPEAKING	▶	changing the topic

UNIT QUESTION

Is one road to success better than another?

A Discuss these questions with your classmates.

1. What does being successful mean to you?

2. In your life, have you taken a traditional path or a non-traditional path to reach your educational and career goals? What are the advantages and disadvantages of each path?

3. Look at the photo. What are these students doing? How can learning a new skill lead to success?

B Listen to *The Q Classroom* online. Then answer these questions.

1. Marcus thinks that different experiences give workers different perspectives. What is an example of this kind of non-traditional path to success?

2. Felix lists many steps on a traditional road to success: studying hard, getting a degree, getting work experience, getting an entry-level job, and working your way up to the top. Which do you think is the most important step? Why?

 C Go to the Online Discussion Board to discuss the Unit Question with your classmates.

127

D Imagine you are meeting with a career counselor to decide what career you want to have. What kind of skills and experiences would help you get the job you desire? Complete the questionnaire below.

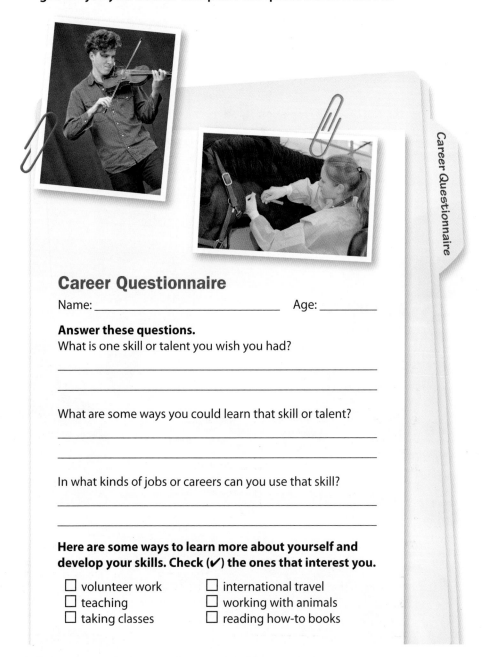

Career Questionnaire

Name: _____ Age: _____

Answer these questions.
What is one skill or talent you wish you had?

_____

_____

What are some ways you could learn that skill or talent?

_____

_____

In what kinds of jobs or careers can you use that skill?

_____

_____

Here are some ways to learn more about yourself and develop your skills. Check (✔) the ones that interest you.

☐ volunteer work   ☐ international travel
☐ teaching   ☐ working with animals
☐ taking classes   ☐ reading how-to books

E Discuss these questions in a group.

1. What are some possible benefits of taking a year off from school or work to do something else? What might the disadvantages be?

2. If you took a year off from school, what kinds of experiences would you seek? Why?

When you hear information about related topics, it can be helpful to build a chart so you can easily compare and contrast the main ideas about each topic. Label the columns of your chart with the topics, and label the rows with the examples. Then write notes about each topic in the appropriate box. This is a great way to review and edit your notes after a lecture and to make connections between lectures and readings.

A. Listen to the class discussion about non-traditional approaches some businesses have taken to success. Complete the chart.

Company	History	Success	Problems
Ben and Jerry's	• • • •	• •	• •
Lululemon	• • •	• •	• •
Starbucks	• •	•	• •

B. Use your notes to write a paragraph comparing and contrasting the companies discussed in the lecture.

C. Go online for more practice building a chart to compare and contrast notes on multiple topics.

LISTENING 1 | Changing Ways to Climb the Ladder

UNIT OBJECTIVE ▶▶▶ You are going to hear an excerpt from a college lecture. In the lecture, a professor compares types of career paths. As you listen to the lecture, gather information and ideas about whether one road to success is better than another.

PREVIEW THE LISTENING

A. PREVIEW Is it better to work for one company for many years or to change companies often in order to make progress in your career? Discuss with a partner. Give reasons for your opinion.

B. VOCABULARY Read aloud these words from Listening 1. Check (✓) the ones you know. Use a dictionary to define any new or unknown words. Then discuss with a partner how the words will relate to the unit.

advancement *(n.)*	climb the ladder *(phr.)*	devote *(v.)* 🔑	radically *(adv.)*
attitude *(n.)* 🔑	count on *(phr. v.)*	loyal *(adj.)* 🔑	stable *(adj.)* 🔑
career path *(n.)*	currently *(adv.)* 🔑	model *(n.)* 🔑	structure *(n.)* 🔑

🔑 Oxford 3000™ words

 C. Go online to listen and practice your pronunciation.

WORK WITH THE LISTENING

A. LISTEN AND TAKE NOTES Listen to the lecture and take notes in the chart.

Model	Path	Advantages	Disadvantages
Traditional model for advancement	• •	• •	•

Model	Path	Advantages	Disadvantages
Modern model for advancement	•	•	•
		•	

B. Which model do you think is better? Discuss your opinion with a partner. Use your notes to defend your choice.

C. Read the statements. Write *T* (true) or *F* (false). Then correct the false statements.

_____ 1. Workers today are most likely to follow the new model in their careers.

_____ 2. The typical career path has not changed much in the last few decades.

_____ 3. The workers are more loyal to their company in the new model.

_____ 4. The new model gives workers more choices about their personal lives.

_____ 5. Some people choose to slow down their career advancement.

D. Listen again. Check (✓) the correct model for each statement.

Detail	Traditional model	New model
1. This model was more common in the 1950s in North America.	☐	☐
2. This model is currently more common in the United States.	☐	☐
3. Workers start at small companies to get experience.	☐	☐
4. Workers start at the bottom level of a big company.	☐	☐
5. Workers are loyal to one company and expect the company to take care of them.	☐	☐
6. Workers are not very loyal to the companies they work for.	☐	☐

Detail	Traditional model	New model
7. Workers are like family in a company.	☐	☐
8. Workers get to the top of the ladder about four years faster.	☐	☐
9. This model is more flexible.	☐	☐
10. Companies don't often take care of workers when they retire.	☐	☐

Vocabulary Skill Review

In Unit 5, you learned to use prefixes and suffixes to help determine the meaning of new vocabulary words. Identify two words containing a suffix used for adverbs in Activity E.

E. VOCABULARY Here are some words from Listening 1. Complete each sentence with the correct word.

advancement (n.)	climb the ladder (phr.)	devote (v.)	radically (adv.)
attitude (n.)	count on (phr. v.)	loyal (adj.)	stable (adj.)
career path (n.)	currently (adv.)	model (n.)	structure (n.)

1. This company is very _____. They have a strong business plan, and they won't go out of business any time soon.

2. I'd like to help you, but I don't have any free time to _____ to anything else right now. I spend all my time working on this project.

3. She has a very negative _____ toward her job. She never has anything good to say about it.

4. After he lost weight, he looked _____ different. It was such a big change that we didn't even recognize him when we saw him.

5. We have to work really hard to finish this project. Our boss is _____ us to finish it before Friday.

6. We are going to examine two different educational systems. Each _____ has advantages and disadvantages.

7. I used to live in New York, but I moved. I _____ live in London, where I plan to stay for a couple of years.

8. I am thinking about accepting a new job, but I need to find out about the opportunities for _____ first. I hope to be promoted soon.

9. Adán is very _____ to our company. He has been offered jobs at other companies, but he always stays here.

10. Our department's _____ is very simple. I report to my boss, and he reports to the company president.

11. In this company, the usual _____ is to go from a salesperson to a senior manager in a few years.

12. It took me many years to _____ at this company. I started in the mailroom and I finally became a vice president last year.

 F. Go online for more practice with the vocabulary.

 ## SAY WHAT YOU THINK

Discuss the questions in a group.

1. Which model of climbing the ladder best matches your personality? Do you think this method would work well in your current or future career?

2. What are some careers that would work well in each model? Give specific reasons for your choices.

Listening Skill | **Listening for contrasting ideas**

When speakers **contrast** things or ideas, they use special words and phrases to point out different characteristics of the things being discussed.

The simplest way to show a contrast is to use a comparative adjective + *than.*

> In fact, jumping up a few steps at a time . . . is actually quite common in this model, and now business leaders are getting to the top an average of four years **faster than** in the days of the traditional model.

Speakers also contrast things and ideas by using phrases such as *in contrast to, instead of, however, on the other hand, but, rather than,* and *whereas.* In Listening 1, the speaker contrasts the traditional model with the new model.

> **In contrast to** the single-ladder model . . .
> **On the other hand**, often the worker is able to move to a position . . .
> In the new model, workers are starting their careers at smaller companies **rather than** bigger ones.

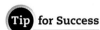

Tip for Success

To understand a speaker's meaning, it's important to analyze the words and phrases they use. The way a speaker organizes and presents information is usually an important clue about what the speaker wants you to know.

A. Listen to a discussion about two candidates for a job. Fill in the blanks with the contrasting words and phrases you hear.

Mr. Doshi: Bob Quintero and Susan Miyamoto are the final candidates for the marketing position at our company. Bob has a degree from Harvard University in the U.S.A., _____ 1 _____ Susan has a degree from Keio Business School in Japan.

Ms. Stanz: Bob and Susan both have good work experience. Bob has worked for five years at a small marketing company, _____ 2 _____ Susan has worked for eight years at our company.

Mr. Doshi: Susan speaks more languages. Bob speaks Arabic and Spanish. _____ 3 _____, Susan speaks French, Spanish, and Japanese.

Ms. Stanz: Bob has a lot of sales experience. _____ 4 _____, Susan has a lot of experience at our company.

Mr Doshi: Hmmm. This is going to be a tough decision!

B. Listen to Listening 1 again. As you listen, complete the chart. Circle *Yes* or *No*.

	Traditional model	New model
1. Are employees loyal?	Yes / No	Yes / No
2. Is the model like a family?	Yes / No	Yes / No
3. Is it a single-ladder model?	Yes / No	Yes / No
4. Can workers advance quickly?	Yes / No	Yes / No
5. Is the model more common today?	Yes / No	Yes / No

 C. Go online for more practice listening for contrasting ideas.

LISTENING 2 | Life Experience Before College

You are going to listen to a radio program about students who take a "gap year," a year off between high school and college. As you listen to the radio program, gather information and ideas about whether one road to success is better than another.

PREVIEW THE LISTENING

Some students go backpacking during their gap year.

A. **PREVIEW** What are some reasons why a student might want to take a year off from school? Discuss with a partner.

B. **VOCABULARY** Read aloud these words from Listening 2. Check (✓) the ones you know. Use a dictionary to define any new or unknown words. Then discuss with a partner how the words will relate to the unit.

commute (n.)	figure (v.) 🔑	point (n.) 🔑
concept (n.) 🔑	log (v.)	rigorous (adj.)
dare (v.) 🔑	particular (adj.) 🔑	serve one well (phr.)
face (v.) 🔑	peer (n.)	stand out (phr. v.)

🔑 Oxford 3000™ words

C. Go online to listen and practice your pronunciation.

WORK WITH THE LISTENING

A. **LISTEN AND TAKE NOTES** Listen to the radio program. Then list the advantages and disadvantages of taking a gap year in the chart.

	Advantages	Disadvantages
Taking a gap year	•	•
		•
	•	
		•

B. Imagine a student wanted to take a gap year, but his or her parents thought starting university right away was a better idea. Work with a partner. Use your notes to write a dialogue between a teenager and a parent about this choice.

C. Read the statements. Write *T* (true) or *F* (false). Then correct the false statements.

____ 1.   Taking a gap year is a familiar concept in the United States.

_____

____ 2.   Gap years give students a chance to do something that really interests them.

_____

____ 3.   Taking a gap year requires a lot of planning.

_____

____ 4.   A gap year can hurt your résumé.

_____

____ 5.   A gap year gives students an experience that many of their classmates in college don't have.

_____

D. Read the questions. Then listen again. Circle the correct answers.

1.   In which country is taking a gap year the least common?
    a.   The United States
    b.   Australia
    c.   Great Britain

2.   How did Antonia House become interested in traveling?
    a.   She studied international relations in high school.
    b.   She graduated from high school in Berlin.
    c.   She spent a summer in France.

3.   How does taking a year off school affect most students' grades?
    a.   Their grades are worse than other students'.
    b.   Their grades are better than other students'.
    c.   Their grades are the same as other students'.

4. Why does the speaker say that you need a lesson plan for a gap year?
   a. Because students should learn a lot from the experience.
   b. Because schools require it.
   c. Because students need to make arrangements ahead of time.

5. What advice does Trudee Goodman have for people interested in taking a gap year?
   a. Live with family members because it will save you money.
   b. Learn as much as possible through your experiences.
   c. Write about the experience on your résumé so you can get a job.

E. Check (✓) the advantages that Trudee Goodman mentions about working in disadvantaged schools.

☐ 1. She was tired of studying.
☐ 2. She had more time for her hobbies.
☐ 3. Her experience felt more real.
☐ 4. She made a lot of new friends.
☐ 5. She already has real-world work experience.
☐ 6. She didn't need to study as hard when she returned to school.

F. VOCABULARY Here are some words from Listening 2. Read the sentences. Then write each bold word next to the correct definition.

1. Taking time off before going to college is a new **concept** for most students in the United States. Many students have never thought about it before.

2. I am too afraid to leave my family, so I wouldn't **dare** travel alone in another country.

3. Many teenagers buy the clothes their friends buy. It's important to them to look like their **peers**.

4. I am not sure what time it is, but the sun is high in the sky, so I **figure** it must be around 12:00 noon.

5. The **point** of the class was to prepare the students for the exam.

6. I am interested in that **particular** English class because I've heard that teacher is very good.

7. My new math class is much more **rigorous** than the last one. There are a lot more tests and the homework assignments are much harder.

8. My father's **commute** takes two hours a day. It takes about an hour to drive between his home and his office.

9. You need to **log** the hours you worked on this sheet. Accurate records help us know how much time the job is taking.

10. Because so many people applied for the job my sister wanted, she had to **face** the possibility that she might not get hired.

11. My brother studied hard. He hoped it would **serve him well** by making it easier to get a good job after graduation.

12. The new student knew she would **stand out** because she didn't have a school uniform yet. She looked completely different from the other students.

a. _____ (*v.*) to think or guess

b. _____ (*phr.*) be an advantage to someone

c. _____ (*adj.*) one specific person, place, thing, or time

d. _____ (*n.*) people who are of the same age or social status

e. _____ (*v.*) to keep a written record of something

f. _____ (*n.*) the trip from home to work every day by car, bus, or train

g. _____ (*phr. v.*) to be easily seen or noticed

h. _____ (*v.*) to be brave enough to do something

i. _____ (*v.*) to deal with something unpleasant

j. _____ (*adj.*) strict or demanding

k. _____ (*n.*) an idea or basic principle

l. _____ (*n.*) the purpose of something

 G. Go online for more practice with the vocabulary.

H. Go online to listen to *Is Pop Culture Making Us Smarter?* and check your comprehension.

SAY WHAT YOU THINK

A. Discuss the questions in a group.

1. If you could go anywhere in the world for a year, where would you go? Why?

2. If a close friend were considering taking off a year between high school and college, what advice would you give your friend?

3. What types of gap year activities could help prepare someone for a career in education? In banking?

B. Before you watch the video, discuss the questions in a group.

1. Would you consider working for free in order to learn more about a job you might want to do in the future? If yes, what job would you like to try?

2. Do you know of anyone who has ever done an internship? What was his or her experience like?

 C. Go online to watch a video about interns. Then check your comprehension.

> **commensurate** *(adj.)* matching something in size, importance, quality, etc.
>
> **disingenuous** *(adj.)* not sincere, especially when you pretend to know less about something than you really do
>
> **exacerbate** *(v.)* make a problem worse
>
> **interns** *(n.)* people, usually students, who often work for free while learning about a job or career
>
> **sue** *(v.)* to make a claim against somebody in court about something that they have said or done to harm you

VIDEO VOCABULARY

D. Think about the unit video, Listening 1, and Listening 2 as you discuss the questions.

1. Think about your education or career. Which have you chosen more often: a traditional or non-traditional path? Why?

2. Has there ever been a time when you wanted to follow a non-traditional path but you didn't? Why didn't you?

English does not have strong rules of formality like some languages do. However, in some situations, it may be more appropriate to use certain words than others. In other more casual situations, it may be more appropriate to use less formal vocabulary, such as *phrasal verbs* and *idioms*. It is helpful to know when to use certain words and phrases.

A dictionary can guide you on which word to use. It will tell you if a word is informal or slang. If a definition doesn't say this, you can usually assume it is more formal or neutral.

Here are some examples.

PHR V ˌhang aˈround (…) (*informal*) to wait or stay near a place, not doing very much: *You hang around here in case he comes, and I'll go on ahead.* ˌhang aˈround with sb (*informal*) to spend a lot of time with someone ˌhang ˈback to remain

so·cial·ize /ˈsouʃəˌlaɪz/ *verb* **1** [I] ~ (**with sb**) to meet and spend time with people in a friendly way, in order to enjoy yourself **SYN** MIX: *I enjoy socializing with the other students.* ◆ *Maybe you should socialize more.* **2** [T, often passive] ~ **sb**

those old photos—they may be valuable. ˌhang ˈout (*informal*) to spend a lot of time in a place: *The local kids hang out at the mall.* ⊃ related noun HANGOUT ˌhang ˈout with sb (*informal*)

The dictionary categorizes *hang around* and *hang out* as informal, but *socialize* has no description like this.

Here are some examples of appropriate use.

To your friends: I'll be <u>hanging around</u> all day.

To your family: I'm going to <u>hang out</u> with my friends today.

In a presentation: Most teenagers enjoy <u>socializing</u> with friends.

All dictionary entries are from the *Oxford Advanced American Dictionary for learners of English* © Oxford University Press 2011.

A. Read the pairs of sentences. Check (✓) the sentence that sounds more formal.

1. ☐ a. I can always **count on** you to help me out.
   ☑ b. I always **trust** that you'll assist me.

2. ☐ a. My brother must **select** a new suit for his interview.
   ☐ b. My brother has to **pick out** a new suit for his interview.

3. ☐ a. Lately I've been **enthusiastic about** volunteering.
   ☐ b. These days **I'm really into** the idea of volunteering.

4. ☐ a. I have to **cut back** on my work hours this semester.
   ☐ b. I have to **reduce** the number of hours I work this semester.

B. Read the sentences. Circle the answer that means almost the same as the bold word in each sentence.

1. I don't think we need to **hang around** here until he returns.
   a. wait
   b. climb
   c. joke

2. He was hoping to **get** a promotion at work.
   a. find
   b. receive
   c. give

3. You don't need to **put up with** a job that is so boring! Get a new one.
   a. tolerate
   b. look for
   c. create

4. Have you **looked into** other companies to work for? There must be many others like that one.
   a. answered
   b. counted
   c. researched

5. **Jumping up** a few steps at a time is almost impossible in a traditional career path.
   a. bouncing
   b. advancing
   c. returning

6. I've been working so hard at school. I'm **worn out**. I need to rest!
   a. prepared
   b. tired
   c. worried

C. Circle the appropriate synonym to complete each sentence. Then work with a partner to read the conversations.

Interviewee: Good morning. I'm here to (have a word / speak) with Mr. Simon.
1

Receptionist: Please (wait / hang around) here. I'll tell Mr. Simon you're here.
2

Mr. Simon: Good morning. So let's (get going / begin). Can you tell me why you'd like to work for this company?
3

Interviewee: Well, I'm really (interested in / into) your products.
4

 D. Go online for more practice with using the dictionary to find formal or informal words.

SPEAKING

UNIT OBJECTIVE
At the end of this unit, you are going to participate in a group discussion about the qualifications of job applicants and make a hiring decision. Throughout the discussion, you will need to be able to change the topic.

Grammar | **Simple, compound, and complex sentences**

Using a variety of sentence types will allow you to express a range of ideas in your speeches and presentations.

There are three basic kinds of sentences: **simple**, **compound**, and **complex**.

A **simple sentence** is one independent clause (one subject + verb combination) that makes sense by itself.

I want to do research.
subject verb

A **compound sentence** is made of at least two independent clauses joined together with a conjunction, such as *for*, *and*, *nor*, *but*, *or*, *yet*, *so*, or *as*.

independent clause   independent clause
The worker went to a new company, and she moved up the ladder faster.
conjunction

A **complex sentence** is made of at least one independent clause and one dependent clause. A dependent clause is not a complete idea by itself. The dependent clause begins with a subordinating conjunction, such as *because*, *since*, *after*, *although*, *if*, or *when*.

independent clause   dependent clause
I looked at the gap year information **before** I gave it to my brother.
subordinating conjunction

If the dependent clause comes before the independent clause, then a comma separates the two clauses.

Although it is less stable, many workers prefer the new career model.

A. Read each sentence. Is the sentence simple, compound, or complex? Circle the correct answer. Then compare answers with a partner.

1. This model is similar to the business cultures in other countries.
   (simple / compound / complex)

2. The right training is important, but what other steps do you need to take to reach your career goal?
   (simple / compound / complex)

3. Because he moved in and out of companies as positions opened, he could move faster toward his career goal.
   (simple / compound / complex)

4. Many countries in Asia follow this business model.
   (simple / compound / complex)

5. After she worked for a year, she was ready to return to school.
   (simple / compound / complex)

B. Rewrite the conversation below. Combine the simple sentences using the words in parentheses. Then practice the conversation.

Sam was walking down the street. He saw his friend Inez. (when)

Sam was walking down the street when he saw his friend Inez.

Inez: Hey, Sam! How did your job interview go?

Sam: Hi! It went really well. I might get the job! (and)

Inez: That's great! When will you know for sure?

Sam: They'll make the decision this afternoon. They'll call me. (after)

Inez: Good luck! By the way, did you hear about Adam?

Sam: No. I sent him an email last week. He hasn't answered it. (but)

Inez: Well, he's taking a year off. He's going to Antarctica to study penguins.
   (because)

Sam: Wow! That sounds amazing.

Inez: Yeah. It seems like an incredible opportunity. I can't imagine living in
   Antarctica. (although)

Sam: What about you? How are you going to spend the summer?

Inez: I applied to two programs. I might volunteer for a group that builds houses for people. I might work in a program for street kids. (or)

Sam: Those both sound like important projects! They'll look good on your college application. (and)

Inez: Yeah. I need to do something significant. I want to get into a good school! (if)

Sam: Well, I should get home. I can wait for the call about the job. (so)

Inez: See you later!

C. Go online for more practice with simple, compound, and complex sentences.

D. Go online for the grammar expansion.

Pronunciation Highlighted words

Speakers typically use a higher pitch and longer vowel sounds to emphasize or highlight content words.

For example, a speaker might stress the words in the following sentence normally.

<u>Colleges</u> say a <u>gap year</u> doesn't <u>have</u> to be <u>costly</u>.

Sometimes a speaker will shift the stress from this regular stress pattern to emphasize an idea. **Highlighted words** often present a contrast or a correction. A speaker who wants to emphasize that taking a gap year can be inexpensive might place a heavier stress on *have*.

<u>Colleges</u> say a <u>gap year</u> doesn't **have** to be <u>costly</u>.

Or, if the speaker wants to communicate that this idea is supported by colleges but not by students, a heavier stress might be shifted to *Colleges*.

Colleges say that a <u>gap year</u> doesn't <u>have</u> to be <u>costly</u>.

A. Listen to each sentence. Underline the highlighted words you hear. Then practice saying the sentences with a partner.

1. I would love to take a gap year to work in India.

2. If I had to pick just one place to go, it would be Turkey.

3. When Carlos was there, they didn't have the volunteer program.

4. Chris and Ilona are going too? Hassan told me they're not going.

5. You'll learn a lot while you're there, and you'll have so much fun!

B. Listen to each sentence. What is the speaker's meaning? Circle the correct answer.

1. I would like to get a job in Africa taking care of wild animals.
   a. I am interested in Africa.
   b. I hope I can get the job.
   c. My main interest is wild animals.

2. I change jobs often. My father's career path was more traditional.
   a. My career path is different from my father's career path.
   b. I like to change jobs to help my career.
   c. I prefer traditional career paths.

3. I think I can build skills for this career if I take a year off to study.
   a. I'm not sure I can build my skills.
   b. I can only build skills by taking time off.
   c. If I take a year off, I have to study the whole time.

4. The best reason to take a gap year is the chance to learn about yourself.
   a. This reason is very important.
   b. Learning is very important.
   c. You are very important.

5. No one ever told me that the group would leave before school is over.
   a. I thought the group was staying at the school.
   b. I thought the group would leave after school is over.
   c. They told other people, but they forgot to tell me.

volunteering at a summer camp

C. Work with a partner. Practice the conversation. Stress the bold words.

A: Have you heard about Lee's **latest** plan?

B: No. What does he want to do **now**?

A: He says he **finally** decided to volunteer at a summer camp.

B: He wants to **volunteer**? I thought he wanted a paying job.

A: Well, it seems he changed his mind **again**.

B: Hmm. He **would** be good at it. He's a natural leader.

A: He's good at **lots** of things, so I'm sure he'll think of more ideas.

B: Yeah. He probably won't figure out where to go until **right** before he leaves!

 D. Go online for more practice with highlighted words.

Speaking Skill | Changing the topic

In the middle of a conversation you may want to **change the topic** a little. However, you don't want to sound like you are uninterested in what someone else is saying. To let someone know you want to add something related to the topic, you can use *transition phrases*. Here are some examples:

By the way . . .
Speaking of (previous topic) . . .
That reminds me . . .

For example, if your friend is talking about a book he finished reading yesterday, you can say, "Oh, speaking of books, did you hear about that new adventure novel?"

Sometimes you remember something in the middle of a conversation that is not at all related to the current topic. It is important to let others know you are about to switch to an unrelated topic. Here are some expressions you can use:

Hold that thought.
Oh, before I forget . . .
Oh, I wanted to tell / ask you . . .

For example, you and two friends are talking about an exhibition. You suddenly remember you wanted to ask them about an important class project. You wait for a short pause in the conversation and then say, "Oh, before I forget, I wanted to ask you if you want to go over the project notes today."

To return to the previous topic, you can then use phrases like these:

But you were saying . . .
Back to (the topic) . . .
Anyway . . .

A. Complete the conversation with the words you hear. Then practice the conversation with a partner.

A: I've had a very long day. I just came from my job.

B: _____, I need to get your résumé. My company is
   ₁

hiring, and you would be perfect for the position.

A: Really? That's great! You make your job sound fun.

B: It is, most of the time. We all get along well at work.

A: Oh, _____ if you have time to help me with
my homework.
2

B: Sure I can. We'll do it after class.

A: _____, I'd love to give you my résumé. I've been
looking for a new job.
3

B: I know. _____, my boss says she's interviewing
people next week. Are you free in the morning?
4

A: I'll make sure I'm available if she calls me.

B: _____. I have to get to my next class. We'll talk
about this later.
5

A: See you.

B. **Work in a group. Discuss the questions. Practice changing and returning to topics.**

1. What does it mean to be successful? How do you define it for yourself?

2. What are the characteristics of a dream job? What steps should someone take—traditional and non-traditional—to get their dream job?

3. What type of person is most likely to achieve his or her dream job?

 C. **Go online for more practice changing the topic.**

 In this assignment, you are going to have a discussion in order to reach a group decision. As you prepare for your discussion, think about the Unit Question, "Is one road to success better than another?" Use information from Listening 1, Listening 2, the unit video, and your work in this unit to support your discussion. Refer to the Self-Assessment checklist on page 150.

CONSIDER THE IDEAS

Complete the activities.

1. Read the following advertisement for a job opening.

GapStaff needs you!

GapStaff is looking for a consultant to join our exciting and energetic team. Consultants are responsible for working with clients to organize their gap year opportunities. Candidates for the job should be well organized, interested in working with students, and passionate about traveling, learning, and volunteering.

The minimum requirements for the position are an undergraduate degree and five years of related work experience.
Travel experience and the ability to speak another language are a plus.

Call 1-888-555-5210

2. Read the information about four people who applied for the GapStaff consultant job. Then listen to their personal statements. Take notes in the chart.

Personal information	Notes

Susan Jones (age 59)
Education:
  A.A. in Journalism from Central Texas College
  B.A. in English from the University of Chicago
Work Experience:
  English teacher in Poland (3 years)
  English teacher in Morocco (2 years)
  English teacher in Peru (6 years)	

Personal information	Notes

Doug Orman (age 43)
Education:
  B.A. in History from the University of Maryland
  M.A. in History from the University of Maryland
Work Experience:
  Teaching Assistant at the University of Maryland (3 years)
  Lecturer at the University of Maryland (16 years)	

Narayan Tej (age 24)
Education:
  B.A. Tourism from Columbia Southern University
Work Experience:
  Part-time work at the tourism desk of the Hilton Hotel	

Teresa Lopez (age 35)
Education:
  B.S. in Business Administration from National
    American University
Work Experience:
  Guide at local museum (3 years)
  Receptionist for travel agent (2 years)
  Receptionist for gym (5 years)
  Salesperson at a clothing store (2 years)	

PREPARE AND SPEAK

A. **GATHER IDEAS** Imagine you are part of a GapStaff group choosing the best candidate for the position. Consider the four job applicants. Who do you think is most qualified? Who is least qualified? Rank the applicants from 1 (your first choice) to 4 (your last choice), based on your notes in the chart above.

____ Susan Jones

____ Doug Orman

____ Narayan Tej

____ Teresa Lopez

Critical Thinking Tip

Activity B asks you to **rank** the candidates. When you rank things, you make a judgment about different characteristics. This is an important higher-level thinking skill.

B. **ORGANIZE IDEAS** Why did you rank the candidates in this order? Complete the chart with brief notes.

Candidate name	Reasons for ranking
1.	
2.	
3.	
4.	

C. **SPEAK** Work in a group. Discuss who should be hired for the position. Share your reasons with the group. Work to reach a group decision on the best person to hire. Refer to the Self-Assessment checklist below before you begin.

 Go online for your alternate Unit Assignment.

CHECK AND REFLECT

A. **CHECK** Think about the Unit Assignment as you complete the Self-Assessment checklist.

SELF-ASSESSMENT		
Yes	No	
☐	☐	I was able to speak easily about the topic.
☐	☐	My partner, group, and class understood me.
☐	☐	I listened for contrasting ideas.
☐	☐	I used vocabulary from the unit.
☐	☐	I changed the topic in the discussion.
☐	☐	I highlighted words to emphasize ideas as I spoke.

 B. **REFLECT** Go to the Online Discussion Board to discuss these questions.

1. What is something new you learned in this unit?

2. Look back at the Unit Question—Is one road to success better than another? Is your answer different now than when you started this unit? If yes, how is it different? Why?

TRACK YOUR SUCCESS

Circle the words and phrases you have learned in this unit.

Nouns
advancement
attitude 🔑 AWL
career path
commute
concept 🔑 AWL
model 🔑
peer
point 🔑
structure 🔑 AWL

Verbs
dare 🔑
devote 🔑 AWL
face 🔑
figure 🔑
log

Phrasal verbs
count on
stand out

Adjectives
loyal 🔑
particular 🔑
rigorous
stable 🔑 AWL

Adverbs
currently 🔑
radically

Phrases
climb the ladder
serve one well

🔑 Oxford 3000™ words
AWL Academic Word List

Check (✓) the skills you learned. If you need more work on a skill, refer to the page(s) in parentheses.

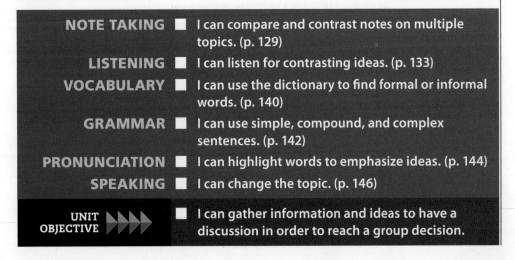

NOTE TAKING	☐ I can compare and contrast notes on multiple topics. (p. 129)
LISTENING	☐ I can listen for contrasting ideas. (p. 133)
VOCABULARY	☐ I can use the dictionary to find formal or informal words. (p. 140)
GRAMMAR	☐ I can use simple, compound, and complex sentences. (p. 142)
PRONUNCIATION	☐ I can highlight words to emphasize ideas. (p. 144)
SPEAKING	☐ I can change the topic. (p. 146)
UNIT OBJECTIVE ▶▶▶▶	☐ I can gather information and ideas to have a discussion in order to reach a group decision.

UNIT 7

Anthropology

LISTENING	▶	listening for signal words and phrases
NOTE TAKING	▶	taking notes on details
VOCABULARY	▶	collocations with prepositions
GRAMMAR	▶	indirect speech
PRONUNCIATION	▶	linked words with vowels
SPEAKING	▶	using questions to maintain listener interest

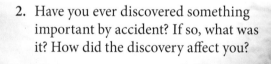

UNIT QUESTION

How can accidental discoveries affect our lives?

A Discuss these questions with your classmates.

1. The journalist Franklin Adams once wrote, "I find that a great part of the information I have was acquired by looking up something and finding something else on the way." What do you think he meant?

2. Have you ever discovered something important by accident? If so, what was it? How did the discovery affect you?

3. Look at the photos. How might each of these discoveries be useful?

UNIT OBJECTIVE Listen to two reports and gather information and ideas to tell a personal story about an accidental discovery you made and how it affected you.

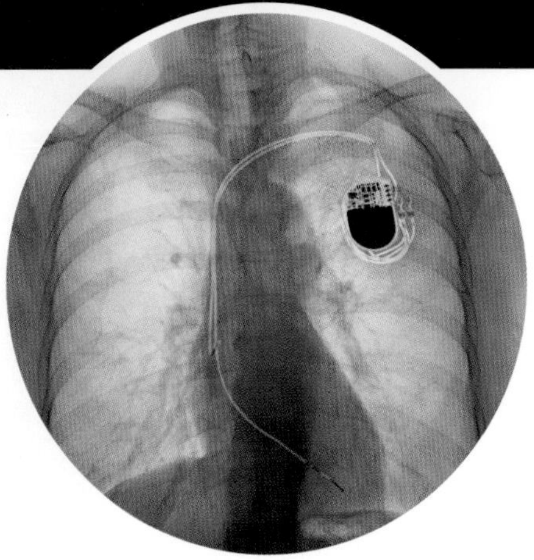

B Listen to *The Q Classroom* online. Then answer these questions.

1. Marcus says that it is important to keep learning and having new experiences. Do you agree with him? What does his advice have to do with making accidental discoveries?
2. Each student talks about accidental discoveries in a very positive way. Do you think there are some situations where accidental discoveries aren't so positive? If so, in what situations?

iQ ONLINE **C Go online to watch the video about a useful product that was invented by accident. Then check your comprehension.**

VIDEO VOCABULARY

frivolous *(adj.)* silly, unnecessary

leverage *(n.)* the ability to influence what people do

steer clear *(phr.)* avoid a person who may cause problems

tack *(n.)* stickiness

iQ ONLINE **D Go to the Online Discussion Board to discuss the Unit Question with your classmates.**

E The products below were all discovered or invented by accident. Check (✓) the three products you think have had the greatest effect on the world. Compare your choices with a partner. Discuss reasons for your choices.

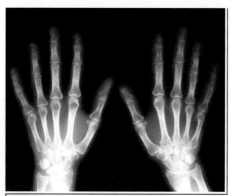
X-ray

potato chips

dynamite

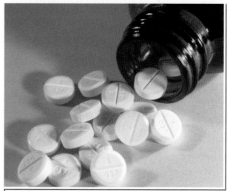
penicillin

microwave oven

plastic

F If you discover something by accident, how do you know if the discovery is important? Discuss with a partner.

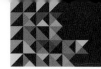

LISTENING

LISTENING 1 | The Power of Serendipity

You are going to listen to a report about how accidents and events led to some important scientific developments. As you listen to the report, gather information and ideas about how accidental discoveries affect our lives.

PREVIEW THE LISTENING

a scientific experiment

A. **PREVIEW** Scientists work hard to keep control of their work and make sure mistakes do not happen. How often do you think accidents play a role in scientific discoveries? Discuss with a partner.

B. **VOCABULARY** Read aloud these words from Listening 1. Check (✓) the ones you know. Use a dictionary to define any new or unknown words. Then discuss with a partner how the words will relate to the unit.

adhesive *(n.)*	inconceivable *(adj.)*	synthetic *(adj.)*
exploit *(v.)*	interact *(v.)*	unreliable *(adj.)*
flammable *(adj.)*	mandatory *(adj.)*	vastly *(adv.)*
inadvertent *(adj.)*	obvious *(adj.)* 🔑	

🔑 Oxford 3000™ words

C. Go online to listen and practice your pronunciation.

WORK WITH THE LISTENING

A. **LISTEN AND TAKE NOTES** Take notes about the main ideas and important details you hear. Use the right side of the chart below and on page 156.

Questions	Notes on main ideas and important details

B. Review your notes from Activity A and write questions in the section on the left. These can be questions you think might be asked by your teacher, questions answered in the listening, or other questions you would like to find answers to. Then compare your notes and questions with a partner.

C. Use your notes to match each scientific breakthrough with the accident or event that led to it. Then listen again to check your answers.

Accident or Event

_____ 1. Alfred Nobel worked with a flammable medicine.

_____ 2. A sticky substance was mixed with sulfur and dropped on a hot stove.

_____ 3. An Ethiopian goat herder watched his goats eating.

_____ 4. Nomads traveled on camels carrying milk in stomach bags.

_____ 5. A scientist tried to invent a new form of adhesive, but it was very weak.

_____ 6. Scientists tried to create synthetic rubber but failed.

Scientific Breakthrough

a. The effects of coffee beans were discovered.

b. Rubber became a useful product.

c. Cheese was made for the first time.

d. Dynamite was discovered.

e. Silly Putty® was invented.

f. Post-It Notes® were invented.

D. Read the statements. Write *T* (true) or *F* (false). Then correct the false sentences.

_____ 1. Serendipity is looking for one thing and finding something more valuable by accident.

_____ 2. Food serendipity has little to do with animals.

_____ 3. Most products we purchase today aren't the result of serendipity.

_____ 4. Serendipity is a source of innovation.

_____ 5. Serendipity is a luxury that is nice but not necessary.

E. Check (✓) the items you think were discovered or invented by accident. Compare your choices with a partner. Then conduct some research to find out if your choices are correct.

1 chocolate chip cookies

2 rechargeable batteries

3 tea

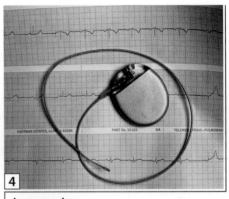

4 the pacemaker

5 Velcro®

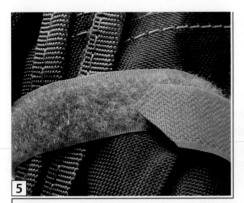

6 GPS (Global Positioning System)

F. VOCABULARY Here are some words from Listening 1. Read the sentences. Circle the answer that best matches the meaning of each bold word.

1. Please keep **flammable** objects away from the stove. It isn't safe while we're cooking.
   a. easily breaks
   b. easily burns

2. My car is **unreliable**. I often have to take the bus to work because my car won't start.
   a. cannot be depended on
   b. cannot be understood

3. Miteb made an **inadvertent** discovery as he drove to the airport. He took the wrong exit, turned left, and was at the airport. Now he's happy he knows a faster route.
   a. not done on purpose
   b. not important to remember

4. Solar energy is a great source of power but not enough people use it. We must learn to **exploit** it more fully.
   a. to use something for benefit
   b. to save something

5. There is an **obvious** connection between getting overtired and getting sick.
   a. hard to understand
   b. easy to see

6. We need a strong **adhesive** to hang the poster on the wall. Otherwise, the poster will just fall off.
   a. glue
   b. surface

7. Not long ago, there was no wireless communication. But now, living without it is **inconceivable** for many people.
   a. hard to find
   b. hard to imagine

8. Nawaf and I have **vastly** different taste in clothes.
   a. hardly
   b. very greatly

9. Many people like to use websites to **interact** with people with similar interests.
   a. find people's contact information
   b. communicate with other people

10. Attendance at our monthly meetings is **mandatory**. Everyone must attend.
    a. exciting
    b. required

11. According to my auto mechanic, **synthetic** oil is better for my car than regular oil. He says man-made oil lasts longer.
    a. not natural
    b. not expensive

 G. Go online for more practice with the vocabulary.

 SAY WHAT YOU THINK

Discuss these questions in a group.

1. Several of the products mentioned in the report were invented by scientists who were working hard to invent something else. What do you think this tells us about serendipity?

2. Some of the research and experiments mentioned in the report are paid for by businesses. Do you think this is a wise investment for the businesses? Why or why not?

3. One speaker in the report says serendipity is mandatory. Do you agree with this? Give reasons to support your answer.

Listening Skill	Listening for signal words and phrases

When you are listening to a speaker and hear a word you don't recognize, continue listening for a definition. Sometimes, speakers will give the meaning of a word they just used. Good speakers use **signal words and phrases** to clarify what they mean. Here are some examples.

> This refers to . . .
> This means . . .
> A(n) _____ is . . .
> What I mean by _____ is . . .
> What is _____? It's . . .
> _____, or _____, . . .

Sometimes speakers say the same idea in a different way to make the meaning clear. Here are some ways that speakers signal they are about to provide an explanation.

What I mean is . . .
In other words . . .
Here's what this means . . .
In simpler terms, this means . . .

Listening for signals like these will help you to understand important words and concepts that speakers introduce.

A. Read and listen to the lecture. Fill in the blanks with the signal words and phrases you hear.

Professor: Many people use a microwave oven every day. How many of you know that the microwave oven was the result of an accident?

During World War II, scientists invented the magnetron,

a magnetron

_____ a kind of electronic tube that
₁
produces microwaves. We're all familiar with microwave ovens, but

_____ a microwave? Well, it's a very short
₂
electromagnetic wave.

Anyway, in 1946, an engineer named Dr. Percy Spencer was standing close to a magnetron he was testing. He suddenly noticed something unusual. He felt something warm in his shirt pocket. He reached in and discovered that the candy bar in his pocket was a hot, chocolaty mess.

_____, the candy bar had melted. Dr. Spencer
₃
was so excited because he realized that microwaves could raise the internal temperature of food. _____, microwaves were able to
₄
cook food from the inside out! And do it very quickly.

Dr. Spencer saw the possibilities here. His next step was to build a metal box into which he fed microwave power that couldn't escape. He put various foods inside the metal box and tested cooking them. In time, he invented something that would revolutionize cooking—the ubiquitous microwave oven. By that _____ that we see microwave ovens just about everywhere.

5

B. **Read the sentences. Complete each sentence with a signal word or phrase from the Listening Skill box. Then practice reading the sentences with a partner.**

1. It was all by accident. _____ the invention was the result of serendipity.

2. There were endless possibilities. _____ the new discovery could be used for many different things.

3. Then a light bulb went off. _____ I realized what I had to do to make it work correctly.

4. It was a stupendous success. _____ it worked better than anyone had hoped.

5. Soon it will be commonplace. _____ everyone will own one and love it!

A light bulb went off.

iQ ONLINE **C.** **Go online for more practice with listening for signal words and phrases.**

Note-taking Skill | Taking notes on details

When you take notes on a report or a story, write down details that are important to the account. Try to list specific names and dates, along with major events and their effects. Do not try to write complete sentences. Instead, just write down key words and phrases to help you remember the details. When you review your notes, the list of details will provide you with a kind of timeline and will help you recall the major people, events, and facts.

A. **Listen and read the account of a major archaeological discovery. Take notes on the important details that make up the story.**

A Walk to Remember

The year was 1940, and Marcel Ravidat was a French 18-year-old. One day he did what he often liked to do. He went for a walk in the woods near his home. He was with two friends and his dog, Robot. They had strolled along those same trails many times, but this day would be different. Marcel would stumble upon something amazing.

Actually, you could say that Robot literally stumbled upon it. Some say that as the group was walking through the woods, the little dog ran off. Marcel and his friends ran after it, trying to keep up. When they finally caught up to Robot, they found him digging down into a hole that had been left by a collapsed tree. And for some reason Marcel began to help Robot dig. He didn't realize that he was about to make a huge archaeological discovery.

The hole he was digging turned out to lead to a system of caves. Marcel climbed down into the cave through the widened hole, and there he found a series of prehistoric wall paintings. There were many of them, and they depicted animals—bulls, horses, and deer—in bright colors.

The discovery became a major news event. Researchers were amazed by it, and tourists flocked to the site from around the world. In fact, so many people visited the cave that in 1963 it had to be closed off again to protect the paintings.

Marcel's discovery was as historic as it was unexpected. When he headed out into those familiar woods that morning, he had no idea that he would find a passageway to another time, to another world.

B. Compare your notes with a partner. Did you miss any important details? Did you list any details that you now think are unnecessary? Use your notes to make a timeline of the main events in the story.

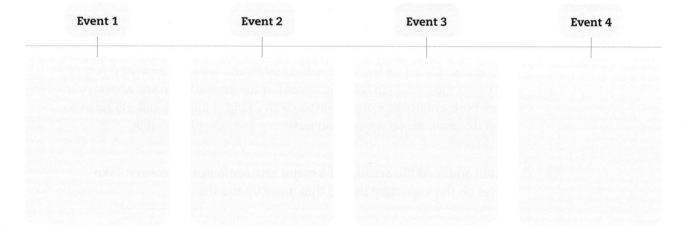

Event 1	Event 2	Event 3	Event 4

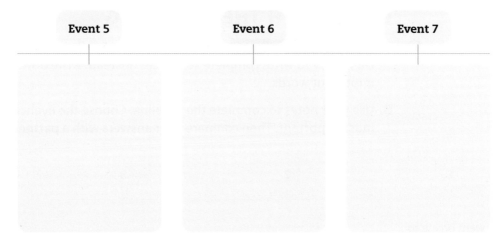

| Event 5 | Event 6 | Event 7 |

 C. Go online for more practice taking notes on details.

LISTENING 2 | Against All Odds, Twin Girls Reunited

 You are going to listen to a report about how twins were reunited unexpectedly. As you listen to the report, gather information and ideas about how accidental discoveries can affect our lives.

PREVIEW THE LISTENING

A. **PREVIEW** If two siblings were separated as babies and then met many years later, do you think they would still feel an emotional connection? Check (✓) *yes* or *no*. Discuss your answer with a partner.

☐ yes
☐ no

B. **VOCABULARY** Read aloud these words from Listening 2. Check (✓) the ones you know. Use a dictionary to define any new or unknown words. Then discuss with a partner how the words will relate to the unit.

ache *(v.)*	biological *(adj.)*	in all probability *(phr.)*
adopt *(v.)* 🔑	deprived *(adj.)*	odds *(n.)*
alert *(adj.)*	face to face *(phr.)*	reunion *(n.)*

🔑 Oxford 3000™ words

 C. Go online to listen and practice your pronunciation.

WORK WITH THE LISTENING

A. **LISTEN AND TAKE NOTES** List the important details you hear in the report. Do not try to write complete sentences. Instead, write down only the important words.

B. Use your notes to complete the timeline. Choose the events you think are most important. Then compare your answers with a partner.

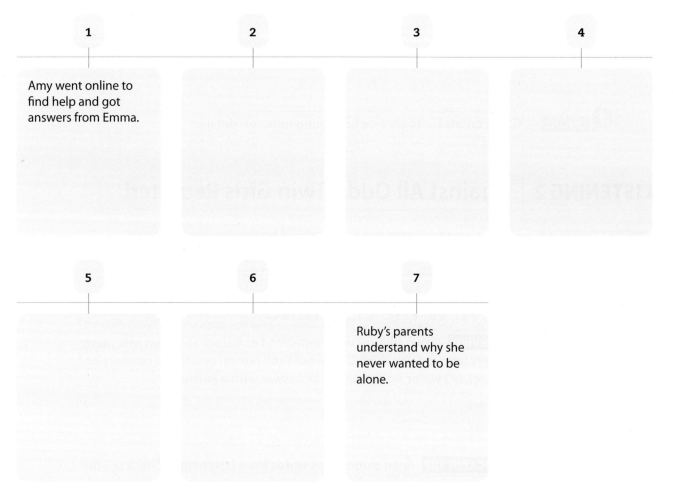

1

Amy went online to find help and got answers from Emma.

2

3

4

5

6

7

Ruby's parents understand why she never wanted to be alone.

C. Listen again. Then answer the questions.

1. How did Emma Smith and Amy White first get to know each other?

   _____

2. Why was Kate's mother, Amy, shocked when she saw the photograph of Ruby?

   _____

3. How did Ruby and Kate get along when they saw each other for the second time at a reunion?

   _____

4. Why did the parents decide to have a DNA test performed?

   _____

5. What did the DNA test results show?

   _____

6. How did Ruby react to the test results?

   _____

D. Read the questions. Circle the correct answers.

1. Where were Ruby and Kate born?
   a. They were born in Florida.
   b. They were born in China.

2. How did Ruby behave when she first went to live with her adoptive parents?
   a. She cried a lot.
   b. She slept a lot.

3. At first, what did Emma Smith believe was the cause of Ruby's behavior?
   a. She believed Ruby was ill.
   b. She believed Ruby was scared.

4. How did Kate behave when she went to live with her new parents?
   a. She ate a lot.
   b. She cried a lot.

5. What advice did Emma Smith give Amy about dealing with Kate's eating problem?
   a. She suggested that they share a plate in the middle of the table.
   b. She suggested that they let Kate eat as much as she wanted.

6. Why did Emma and Amy exchange photographs of their daughters?
   a. They noticed that their daughters shared the same date of birth.
   b. They noticed that their daughters were from the same orphanage.

7. What reason do Ruby and Kate give for why they would like to live next door to each other?

a. They want to go to the same school.

b. They want to play together.

8. According to Emma Smith, why did Ruby never want to be alone?

a. She was scared of her new parents.

b. She had never been alone, even before she was born.

Vocabulary Skill Review

In Unit 4, you learned that in some cases, different parts of speech of a word have the same form. For example, *ache* is spelled the same when it is used as a noun and as a verb. Find two other vocabulary words from Activity E that stay the same in different parts of speech.

E. **VOCABULARY** Here are some words from Listening 2. Complete each sentence with the correct word.

ache *(v.)*	biological *(adj.)*	in all probability *(phr.)*
adopt *(v.)*	deprived *(adj.)*	odds *(n.)*
alert *(adj.)*	face to face *(phr.)*	reunion *(n.)*

1. Amy and Ed have one son. Next year they want to _____ another baby boy. Then they will have two sons.

2. I'm looking forward to our class _____. I haven't seen my classmates in so many years!

3. Derek is usually late to class. _____, he'll be late today as well.

4. My brother may be adopted, but I feel like he's my _____ brother.

5. Ever since Lisa was a baby, she has been very _____. She seems to notice everything that happens around her.

6. Eric was in a serious car accident, but the _____ that he will recover completely are very good.

7. I think I'm getting old. Every morning my knees _____, and my back hurts, too.

8. Although we have texted and emailed each other many times, Janet and I have never met _____. I hope I get to meet her someday.

9. Lucas was born in a very poor city and was _____ of many things. He rarely had a home to sleep in.

F. Go online for more practice with the vocabulary.

G. Go online to listen to *An Unlikely Discovery* and check your comprehension.

 SAY WHAT YOU THINK

A. Discuss the questions in a group.

1. Do you think it is a good idea to encourage the relationship between the two sisters? If so, do you think these families are doing enough to help the sisters?

2. According to the mothers, the girls seemed to "remember" each other and have a natural bond. How would you explain the girls' immediate relationship?

B. Think about the unit video, Listening 1, and Listening 2 as you discuss the questions.

1. In the unit video and Listening 1 you heard about some scientific discoveries that resulted from accidents. In Listening 2 you heard about a personal discovery that was made when two strangers made contact online. Do you think all these discoveries were really accidental? What other factors may have helped lead to these discoveries?

2. Can you think of any ways in which accidental discoveries may have a negative effect on our lives? Discuss any examples you can think of. Consider both scientific discoveries and personal discoveries.

Collocations are combinations of words that are used together frequently. For example, some adjectives and verbs are commonly used with particular prepositions. Part of learning to use these adjectives and verbs correctly involves knowing which prepositions are often used with them.

Here are a few **adjective + preposition** collocations.

embarrassed about	happy about	ready for
fond of	proud of	upset about

Here are a few **verb + preposition** collocations.

complain about	believe in	decide on
arrive at	trip over	approve of

Some collocations are *separable*. A direct object can come between the verb and the preposition.

bring the twins **together**   **combine** the rubber **with** sulfur

Paying attention to collocations will help you develop your fluency because you will know which words to use together.

A. Listen to these sentences. Circle the prepositions that you hear.

Tip for Success

Look up verbs and adjectives in a collocations dictionary to find out which prepositions they are commonly used with.

1. She was looking around, and she was very aware _____ what was going on.
   a. for
   b. over
   c. of

2. Since it's important _____ Kate, I think it's important to all of us.
   a. at
   b. for
   c. to

3. Because we hardly ever fight, and we agree _____ a lot of things.
   a. about
   b. on
   c. in

4. My daughter has not asked me a single question about her birth family or

searching _____ them since she's got Kate in her life.
a. with
b. about
c. for

B. Read the sentences. Complete each sentence with a collocation from the box.

afraid of	stumbling over
filled ___ with	mixed ___ with

1. The idea is to have them interact in open play-like environments, to

encourage them not to be _____ failure, and to

build together.

2. Serendipity refers to looking for one thing and

_____ something else.

3. Rubber was an unreliable, smelly mess until Charles Goodyear

_____ it _____ sulfur.

4. Nomads _____ bags _____ milk and hung

them from their saddles as they rode live camels.

 C. Go online for more practice using collocations with prepositions.

SPEAKING

 At the end of this unit, you are going to tell a personal story about an accidental discovery you made and how it affected you. As you tell the story, you will need to use questions to maintain listener interest.

Grammar | Indirect speech

Direct speech reports what someone said using the speaker's exact words.

☐ The teacher said, "You will have a test on Friday."

Indirect speech also reports what someone said, but without using the speaker's exact words.

☐ The teacher said we would have a test on Friday.

When using indirect speech to report what a speaker said in the past, the verb the speaker used must be changed to a past form.

> **Direct speech:** Moss said, "The whole idea **is** to bring together people with vastly different backgrounds."
> **Indirect speech:** Moss said the whole idea **was** to bring together people with vastly different backgrounds.

When using indirect speech to report a *yes/no* question, use *if* or *whether*.

> **Direct speech:** Kate asked her mother, "Is Ruby from China?"
> **Indirect speech:** Kate asked her mother **if** Ruby was from China.

When using indirect speech to report a *wh-* question, use the same *wh-* word as the speaker.

> **Direct speech:** He asked the professor, "**When** was the microwave oven developed?"
> **Indirect speech:** He asked the professor **when** the microwave oven was developed.

When using indirect speech to report someone's belief, it is not necessary to shift the verb to a past form.

> **Direct speech:** Kate said, "**It's** fun being with Ruby."
> **Indirect speech:** Kate said that **it's** fun being with Ruby.

A. Listen to each sentence. Is it direct or indirect speech? Circle the correct answers.

1. a. direct b. indirect   5. a. direct b. indirect
2. a. direct b. indirect   6. a. direct b. indirect
3. a. direct b. indirect   7. a. direct b. indirect
4. a. direct b. indirect   8. a. direct b. indirect

B. Read these sentences. Rewrite each sentence, changing the direct speech to indirect speech. Then work with a partner to practice saying both versions of each sentence.

1. Mary Tanner said, "The list of serendipity stories is as long as the history of discovery."

_____

_____

2. The professor said, "Many people use a microwave oven every day."

_____

3. The professor said, "He invented something that would revolutionize cooking."

_____

_____

4. The professor said, "We see microwave ovens just about everywhere."

_____

5. Amy said, "I was shocked."

_____

6. Ruby said, "The hole in my heart is getting smaller."

_____

7. Ruby said, "I am Kate," and Kate said, "I am Ruby."

_____

8. In her message, Emma said, "I don't know if my baby knows Amy's baby."

_____

_____

C. Go online for more practice with indirect speech.

D. Go online for the grammar expansion.

Pronunciation | Linked words with vowels

Speakers often link words together so that the last sound in one word connects to the first sound in the next word. Sometimes it's difficult to tell where one word ends and another word begins.

When words ending with the vowel sounds *-ee, -ey, -ah,* and *-oh* are followed by a word beginning with a vowel, the vowels in the two words link together with the /y/ sound. Because the words are pronounced with no pause in between them, it may sound like the second word begins with /y/.

Listen to these sentences and notice how the bold words link with a /y/ sound.

> **She always** wants to **say it**.
>
> Tell me **why it's** important to **be early**.

When words ending with the vowel sounds *-oo, -oh,* and *-ah* are followed by a word beginning with a vowel, the vowels link together with the /w/ sound. Because the words are pronounced with no pause in between them, it may sound like the second word begins with /w/.

Listen to these sentences and notice how the bold words link with a /w/ sound.

> Can she **go out** with us?
>
> Please **show us** your **new invention**.

Linking words is an important part of fluent pronunciation. Practicing this skill will help to make your speech sound more natural.

A. Listen to these pairs of words. Then repeat the words.

1. early age
2. very alert
3. stay awake
4. fly out
5. you opened
6. know about
7. go over
8. how interesting

B. Listen to these sentences. Draw a line to show where the vowels link together. Write *y* or *w* between the words to show the linking sound. Then practice saying the sentences with a partner.

1. Kate also seemed very deprived, because they noticed she ate as if she'd never eat again.

2. After the fact, serendipity always seems so obvious.

3. Because we hardly ever fight, we agree on a lot of things.

4. Try and spot the next big thing.

5. So after you opened the file, can you recall how it felt?

 C. Go online for more practice using linked words with vowels.

Speaking Skill | Using questions to maintain listener interest

When giving a presentation or telling a story, you can keep listeners interested by asking them questions. At the beginning of a presentation, a question can spark interest in your topic. During a presentation, a question can help maintain interest. At the end of your presentation, a question encourages your listeners to keep thinking about your topic after you are done speaking.

There are two main types of questions that speakers ask an audience.

Rhetorical questions are questions that do not require an answer from the audience. Use them to get your listeners to think about what you are about to say.

> What was the most important invention of the twentieth century?
> We all might not agree, but today I'd like to talk to you about one
>   very important invention . . .

Interactive questions are questions for which you expect an answer. Use them to interact with your listeners and encourage them to respond to what you are saying.

> **Presenter:** Does anyone know who discovered the law of gravity?
> **Audience member:** I think it was Isaac Newton.
> **Presenter:** That's right. And the story behind that discovery is an
>   interesting one . . .

Using questions when you present is an effective way to keep the audience paying attention and to help them remember your most important points.

A. Listen to the excerpts from lectures. Which questions are rhetorical and which are interactive? Circle the correct answers.

1. rhetorical   interactive

2. rhetorical   interactive

3. rhetorical   interactive

4. rhetorical   interactive

B. Listen to this short story about another accidental invention. Then answer the questions.

The Popsicle™

The Popsicle™ is a popular summertime treat in the United States. Kids have been enjoying them for decades. But most people don't know that the Popsicle™ was invented by an 11-year-old.

In 1905, Frank Epperson filled a cup with water and fruit-flavored "soda powder," a mix that was used to make a popular drink. Frank left his drink outside on his porch with a stir stick in it. He forgot all about it and went to bed. That night, the temperature dropped to below freezing in San Francisco, where Frank lived. When he woke up the next morning, he discovered that his fruit drink had frozen to the stir stick. He pulled the frozen mixture out of the cup by the stick, creating a fruit-flavored ice treat.

In 1923, Frank Epperson began making and selling his ice treats in different flavors. By 1928, Frank had sold over 60 million Popsicles™, and his business had made him very wealthy. Nowadays, over three million Popsicles™ are sold each year.

Popsicles™ aren't the only invention made by accident. But they might be the tastiest.

Tip for Success

When asking interactive questions, make sure to give your listeners enough time to answer.

1. Which of these would be the most appropriate rhetorical question to start a presentation about this story?
   a. What is one of the tastiest treats ever invented?
   b. What year did Frank Epperson sell his first Popsicle™?
   c. What is the number of Popsicles™ sold every year?

2. Which of these would be the most appropriate interactive question to ask about how Frank Epperson discovered his frozen treat?
   a. What was Frank's favorite flavor of soda water?
   b. What city did Frank live in?
   c. What do you think Frank found the next morning when he went outside?

3. Which of these would be the most appropriate question to ask at the conclusion of your presentation?
   a. Why did Frank choose the name Popsicle™?
   b. Doesn't a Popsicle™ sound tasty right now?
   c. Which is the most popular flavor?

C. In a group, practice telling the story in Activity B in your own words. Use questions to keep your listeners' interest.

D. Go online for more practice with using questions to maintain listener interest.

In this assignment, you are going to tell a personal story about an accidental discovery you made and how it affected you. As you prepare your story, think about the Unit Question, "How can accidental discoveries affect our lives?" Use information from Listening 1, Listening 2, the unit video, and your work in this unit to support your story. Refer to the Self-Assessment checklist on page 176.

CONSIDER THE IDEAS

Look at the list of ideas about discovery. Choose the four ideas you think are the most important factors in making any kind of discovery. Then discuss your answers and reasons with a partner.

desire to succeed	making difficult choices	tools and resources
fortunate accidents	previous experience	trying new things
intelligence	self-confidence	
supportive people	time	

PREPARE AND SPEAK

A. **GATHER IDEAS** Think about your discussion in the Consider the Ideas activity. Write down some brief notes on what you discussed. Include reasons that support your ideas.

Important Ideas about Accidental Discoveries

_____

_____

_____

_____

_____

_____

Critical Thinking Tip

In Activity B, you have to **combine** your ideas from Activity A with the specifics of your experience. Putting ideas together in a new way shows you understand material and can think creatively.

B. **ORGANIZE IDEAS** Think of a personal discovery in your life. For example, think about a time when you discovered you had a talent for a sport or a subject in school. If you can't think of a personal discovery, borrow one from someone else's life experience.

1. How do the ideas in your notes from Activity A apply to this discovery?

2. Make notes about the major events involved in the discovery. List them in the order they happened. Say how this discovery affected you.

Personal discovery:	
Event	**Detail**
Effect:	

C. SPEAK Use your notes to present your story. Remember to explain the steps in how the discovery occurred and how it affected you. As you tell your story, use one or more questions to maintain the interest of your listeners. Refer to the Self-Assessment checklist below before you begin.

 Go online for your alternate Unit Assignment.

CHECK AND REFLECT

A. CHECK Think about the Unit Assignment as you complete the Self-Assessment checklist.

		SELF-ASSESSMENT
Yes	**No**	
☐	☐	I was able to speak easily about the topic.
☐	☐	My partner, group, and class understood me.
☐	☐	I used signal words.
☐	☐	I used vocabulary from the unit.
☐	☐	I used questions to maintain listeners' interest.
☐	☐	I linked words with vowels.

B. **REFLECT** Go to the Online Discussion Board to discuss these questions.

1. What is something new you learned in this unit?

2. Look back at the Unit Question—How can accidental discoveries affect our lives? Is your answer different now than when you started this unit? If yes, how is it different? Why?

TRACK YOUR SUCCESS

Circle the words and phrases you have learned in this unit.

Nouns	Verbs	
adhesive	ache	inconceivable AWL
odds AWL	adopt 🔑	mandatory
reunion	exploit AWL	obvious 🔑 AWL
	interact AWL	synthetic
		unreliable AWL
	Adjectives	**Adverb**
	alert	vastly
	biological	**Phrases**
	deprived	face to face
	flammable	in all probability
	inadvertent	

🔑 Oxford 3000™ words

AWL Academic Word List

Check (✓) the skills you learned. If you need more work on a skill, refer to the page(s) in parentheses.

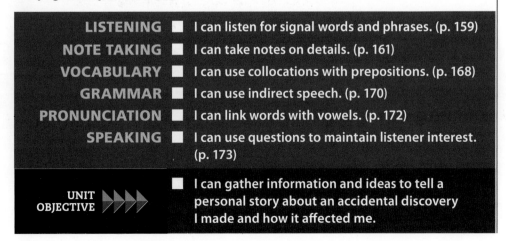

LISTENING ■	I can listen for signal words and phrases. (p. 159)
NOTE TAKING ■	I can take notes on details. (p. 161)
VOCABULARY ■	I can use collocations with prepositions. (p. 168)
GRAMMAR ■	I can use indirect speech. (p. 170)
PRONUNCIATION ■	I can link words with vowels. (p. 172)
SPEAKING ■	I can use questions to maintain listener interest. (p. 173)
UNIT OBJECTIVE ▶▶▶ ■	I can gather information and ideas to tell a personal story about an accidental discovery I made and how it affected me.

UNIT 8

Social Psychology

LISTENING	▶	listening for causes and effects
NOTE TAKING	▶	taking notes on causes and effects
VOCABULARY	▶	idioms
GRAMMAR	▶	uses of real conditionals
PRONUNCIATION	▶	thought groups
SPEAKING	▶	adding to another speaker's comments

UNIT QUESTION

Is athletic competition good for children?

A Discuss these questions with your classmates.

1. Did you play sports or games as a child? If so, what were they? Did you enjoy them? Why or why not?

2. If a child hopes to be a professional athlete, what are the most important things that the child and his or her parents must do to achieve that goal?

3. Look at the photo. What are the positive and negative effects of competition? Is this type of competition good for children?

B Listen to *The Q Classroom* online. Then answer these questions.

1. Marcus says that exercise "gets kids off the sofa and away from their computers and TVs." Do you think this is important? Why or why not?

2. Sophy notes that athletic competition teaches children "self-discipline." What does she mean? What is self-discipline, and how does athletic competition teach this skill?

 C Go to the Online Discussion Board to discuss the Unit Question with your classmates.

D Many young children participate in organized sports. Check (✓) whether each outcome is a benefit, a disadvantage, or neither.

How Do Organized Sports Affect Children?	Benefit	Disadvantage	Neither
getting exercise	☐	☐	☐
the risk of injury	☐	☐	☐
needing to practice	☐	☐	☐
making new friends	☐	☐	☐
time away from schoolwork	☐	☐	☐
building confidence	☐	☐	☐
learning new skills	☐	☐	☐

E Put a check (✓) next to the sport you think is best for young children to participate in. Then work with a partner to compare answers. Give reasons for your answer.

☐ gymnastics
☐ soccer
☐ basketball
☐ martial arts
☐ swimming
☐ another sport: _____

LISTENING

LISTENING 1 | Training Chinese Athletes

UNIT OBJECTIVE

You are going to listen to an interview about young athletes in China. It explains how children are selected and trained to be future gymnastics champions. As you listen to the interview, gather information and ideas about whether or not athletic competition is good for children.

PREVIEW THE LISTENING

A. **PREVIEW** What do you think are important qualities for a champion athlete? Check (✓) the qualities that you agree with. Then discuss your answers with a partner.

☐ physical strength
☐ intelligence
☐ commitment
☐ youth
☐ speed

B. **VOCABULARY** Read aloud these words from Listening 1. Check (✓) the ones you know. Use a dictionary to define any new or unknown words. Then discuss with a partner how the words will relate to the unit.

apex *(n.)*	era *(n.)* 🔑
beneficiary *(n.)*	funding *(n.)*
brutal *(adj.)*	integral *(adj.)*
collapse *(v.)* 🔑	intensity *(n.)*
conclude *(v.)* 🔑	invest *(v.)* 🔑
dominate *(v.)* 🔑	modest *(adj.)*

🔑 Oxford 3000™ words

C. Go online to listen and practice your pronunciation.

WORK WITH THE LISTENING

A. **LISTEN AND TAKE NOTES** Listen to the interview and use the chart to take notes on the different benefits of the athletic training systems in the United States and in China.

Benefits of training system in the United States	Benefits of training system in China

B. Work with a partner. Use your notes to discuss which training system you think is best for the child athletes. Also discuss which system you think is best for the success of the national teams.

C. Check (✓) the events that Jacinta Muñoz experienced according to the interview. Then number the events in the order they happened. Compare your answers with a partner.

____ ☐ trained as a gymnast

____ ☐ became a gymnastics coach

____ ☐ made the United States Olympic Team

____ ☐ won an Olympic medal

____ ☐ retired from gymnastic competition

____ ☐ spent several months in China

____ ☐ injured her knee

____ ☐ competed in the Olympics

D. Listen to the interview again. Circle the answer that best completes each statement.

1. Jacinta Muñoz wanted to learn more about the Chinese system for training athletes because of ____.
   a. the age of the athletes
   b. their recent rise in dominance
   c. the time she spent in China

2. According to the report, funding to support the sports system in China comes from ____.
   a. the athletes
   b the parents
   c. the government

3. Jacinta Muñoz thinks Chinese children are different from American children mainly because Chinese children ____.
   a. are taught to share, not to stand out
   b. want to train harder for sports
   c. train to go to the Olympics

4. Young Chinese athletes are beneficiaries of the Chinese training system because they ____.
   a. receive housing, food, and training
   b. make many sacrifices
   c. learn to share

5. China is also a beneficiary of this training system because ____.
   a. there are Chinese athletes in many sports
   b. it can provide travel to rural children
   c. it has begun a new era of Chinese sports

E. Read the statements. Write *T* (true) or *F* (false). Then correct the false statements.

____ 1. As a young gymnast, Jacinta Muñoz's goal was to become a professional athlete.

_____

____ 2. Jacinta Muñoz quit gymnastics because of the brutal training.

_____

____ 3. Young athletes in China don't see their parents often.

_____

_____ 4. Young athletes in the United States usually get funding from their parents or businesses.

_____

_____ 5. Chinese athletes get free health care and sports training.

_____

_____ 6. Susan Brownell was a gymnastics coach in China and in the United States.

_____

_____ 7. According to the interview, Chinese children are selected based on how good they are in a sport.

_____

Vocabulary
Skill Review

Remember to use context to figure out the meaning of a word that is new to you. The sentence in which the word appears and even the text as a whole may contain clues about the word's meaning.

F. VOCABULARY Here are some words from Listening 1. Read the sentences. Then write each bold word next to the correct definition.

1. Our school's basketball team started to **dominate** the game last Friday in the first few minutes. The other team was able to score very few points.

2. The writer was very **modest**. She didn't like to talk about how famous she had become.

3. Runners sometimes become exhausted and **collapse** before they reach the finish line.

4. The talented ice skater reached the **apex** of his career at age 18. He never won a competition after that.

5. The competition was **brutal**, and some of the athletes had a hard time dealing with the stress and sore muscles.

6. Very good athletes usually have a high level of **intensity** when they compete. They focus all their energy on the sport.

7. The team needed more **funding** to pay for new uniforms.

8. Although you're a talented athlete, you should also **invest** your energy in getting a good education.

9. Eating well is an **integral** part of any fitness program. It's one of my main strategies to stay in shape.

10. After speaking with my advisor, I **concluded** that law school wasn't the right choice for me.

11. I've been the **beneficiary** of my father's hard work. For one thing, he paid for me to go to college.

12. My grandparents grew up in an **era** before the Internet.

a. _____ (n.) a defined period of time in history

b. _____ (adj.) being an important, basic part of something

c. _____ (n.) the highest or best part of something

d. _____ (adj.) extremely difficult and painful

e. _____ (v.) to fall down suddenly

f. _____ (v.) to have more power or skill and to control someone or something with it

g. _____ (n.) a quality of great strength or seriousness

h. _____ (n.) a person or group who gains (usually money) as a result of something

i. _____ (n.) money given to support an event, program, or organization

j. _____ (v.) to put money, effort, time, etc., into something good or useful

k. _____ (v.) to reach a belief or opinion as a result of thought or study

l. _____ (adj.) not talking much about one's own abilities or possessions

 G. Go online for more practice with the vocabulary.

SAY WHAT YOU THINK

Discuss the questions in a group.

Critical Thinking **Tip**

This activity asks you to **appraise** different approaches in the United States and in China. When you make an appraisal or judgment, you evaluate the information from many angles. This demonstrates a deeper understanding of the material.

1. In the United States, parents often spend a lot of money to help their children become better athletes. In China, parents send their children away to school and often don't see them for a long time. Why do you think parents make these kinds of sacrifices?

2. Jacinta Muñoz talks about Susan Brownell's idea that in the United States parents raise their children to succeed and train them to share, but in China they raise their children to share and train them to succeed. Do you think one approach produces better results than the other? Why or why not?

Listening Skill | Listening for causes and effects

A speaker may talk about what **causes** something to happen or what **happens because of** some other action or event. Speakers usually use **signal words** that connect two events or ideas.

These are some of the signal words that speakers use to show a **cause**.

because (of)	as a result of	due to	since	by

Many athletes are driven **by** the hope of winning medals at the Olympics.

The athlete won two gold medals **as a result of** years of hard work.

Due to bad weather, the baseball tournament was canceled.

These are some of the signal words that speakers use to show a **result**.

because of this / that	as a result	therefore	so	the result is

The kids live far from home and practice very hard.
Therefore, they only see their parents every few months.

Some kids start playing some sports too young.
The result is they often get injured before they even reach high school.

Knowing these words and phrases will help you understand how the information is organized and predict what a speaker will say next.

A. Listen to the sentences. Circle the word or phrase you hear in each sentence.

1. a. as a result of
   b. the result is

2. a. therefore
   b. because of this

3. a. because of
   b. due to

4. a. as a result
   b. the result is

5. a. therefore
   b. because

6. a. since
   b. now that

B. Read each sentence. Is the underlined section the *cause* or the *effect*? Write *C* (cause) or *E* (effect).

Tip for Success

When listening to a presentation that mentions causes and effects, mark each cause or effect in your notes. Label them with a *C* or an *E*. This will help you make important connections when you review.

_____ 1. Our team won the game because of our hard work and practice.

_____ 2. Due to a knee injury, Stephan will not be at the track meet this weekend.

_____ 3. Kwan was late to our last competition, so our coach made him sit out this one, too.

_____ 4. Sultan is a better kicker than I am. Therefore, he will start in the soccer game tomorrow.

_____ 5. I will have to miss my brother's baseball game as a result of my busy class schedule.

_____ 6. Since Eduardo couldn't make it today, I will take his place on the team.

iQ ONLINE **C. Go online for more practice with listening for causes and effects.**

| Note-taking Skill | Taking notes on causes and effects |

When you are listening to a report, lecture, or any kind of presentation that deals with causes and effects, list the causes and effects separately. One way to do this is by using a T-chart. Write causes on one side of the chart and effects on the other side. This will help you understand how the causes and effects relate to each other, and it will make reviewing your notes easier.

A. Read this section of a lecture on the benefits of exercise for children. Circle any words or phrases that you think signal causes and effects.

> Most small children love to run and play. But what they don't know is that by playing, they are actually getting smarter. In fact, when kids engage in sports, the results can be long-lasting improvements to their young, developing brains. For instance, a study conducted in 2007 found that vigorous exercise increases the flow of blood to the brain. As a result of this increased blood flow, children who exercise may find it easier to stay alert, focus, and learn. More recent research has also shown that vigorous physical activity helps create new brain cells, therefore causing improved short-term memory and more creativity. In other words, children can become better, more creative students by simply playing hard. School-aged children are often under a great deal of pressure. Some studies have shown that running outdoors actually reduces stress and helps kids deal with many of the pressures they are facing.

B. Complete the student's notes by writing down the missing causes and effects.

Causes	Effects
1.	- getting smarter
2.	- long-lasting effects on brain
3. more blood flow to brain	-
4. create new brain cells	-
5.	- playing hard
6. running outdoors	-

 C. Go online for more practice taking notes on causes and effects.

LISTENING 2 | *Until It Hurts* Discusses Youth Sports Obsession

UNIT OBJECTIVE You are going to listen to a sports journalist and his views on youth sports today. He discusses a recent book by Mark Hyman called *Until It Hurts*. As you listen to the report, gather information and ideas about whether or not athletic competition is good for children.

PREVIEW THE LISTENING

A. **PREVIEW** The book *Until It Hurts* discusses how parents and children can take sports too seriously. Do you think sports should be a major focus of a child's life? Why or why not? Discuss with a partner.

B. **VOCABULARY** Read aloud these words from Listening 2. Check (✓) the ones you know. Use a dictionary to define any new or unknown words. Then discuss with a partner how the words will relate to the unit.

ambition (n.) 🔑	fundamental (adj.) 🔑	regret (v.) 🔑
burnout (n.)	journalist (n.) 🔑	spectator (n.)
escalate (v.)	obsession (n.)	ultimately (adv.) 🔑
former (adj.) 🔑	reasonable (adj.) 🔑	vulnerable (adj.)

🔑 Oxford 3000™ words

 C. Go online to listen and practice your pronunciation.

WORK WITH THE LISTENING

A. **LISTEN AND TAKE NOTES** Listen to the report and complete the chart. Then compare your chart with a partner.

Major changes in youth sports	Negative effects of these changes
1.	1.
2.	2.

B. Read the sentences. Circle the answer that best completes each statement.

1. The sports journalist describes an event in which a father ____.
   a. screamed at the team
   b. fought a referee
   c. got into a fight with another parent

2. According to the book, youth sports used to be run by ____.
   a. children
   b. parents
   c. educators

3. Mark Hyman mentions that playing competitive sports at very young ages can result in ____.
   a. bone fractures
   b. depression
   c. bad grades at school

4. When Mr. Hyman's son Ben complained about his shoulder, Mr. Hyman ____.
   a. forced him to stop playing
   b. encouraged him to keep playing
   c. talked to a doctor

5. Years later, when Ben injured his pitching arm, ____.
   a. he continued playing baseball
   b. he had surgery
   c. he quit playing for years

6. During games in one community, there's a rule banning ____.
   a. talking during games on Sundays
   b. eating food in the stands
   c. more than one parent from each family

C. Listen again. According to Mark Hyman, what are four steps we can take to improve youth sports?

Suggested steps
1.
2.
3.
4.

D. What do you think would be the effects of the changes Mark Hyman suggests? List them below and discuss them with a partner.

Effects of suggested steps
1.
2.
3.
4.

E. **VOCABULARY** Here are some words from Listening 2. Complete each sentence with the correct word.

ambition (n.)	former (adj.)	obsession (n.)	spectator (n.)
burnout (n.)	fundamental (adj.)	reasonable (adj.)	ultimately (adv.)
escalate (v.)	journalist (n.)	regret (v.)	vulnerable (adj.)

1. Mark's first job as a _____ was writing for an online magazine.

2. History has become a(n) _____ for Lindsey. It's all she talks about.

3. After Oscar developed the _____ skills he needed to become a swimmer, his trainer started working on more advanced skills.

4. When we are tired and overworked, we are especially

   _____ to sicknesses like the flu.

5. After weeks of working long hours and getting little sleep, Saud was

   suffering from _____, and he couldn't continue.

6. Thomas was not always a lawyer. In a _____ career, he was

   a professional football player.

7. Abdullah's highest _____ is to be a gold medalist at the

   Olympics, and he believes that he can do it.

8. I considered many universities, but _____ this one proved

   to be the right school for me.

9. A _____ at the game jumped up and cheered loudly as her

   team won the game.

10. It didn't seem _____ for the coach to expect the team to

    practice four hours every day.

11. Quitting the team was a big mistake. It has been many years, and I still

    _____ it.

12. The players' slight disagreement quickly began to _____

    into a big fight.

 F. Go online for more practice with the vocabulary.

G. Go online to listen to *A Child's Dream Helps a Village* **and check your comprehension.**

 SAY WHAT YOU THINK

A. Discuss the questions in a group.

1. Why do you think parents get their children involved in competitive sports at as young as four or five years old? Do you think they should wait until their children are older?

2. Why do you think some parents become obsessed with youth sports and even lose control at their children's games? What advice would you give to these parents?

B. Before you watch the video, discuss the questions in a group.

1. Do you think it is acceptable for parents to strongly encourage their children to participate in some form of organized sports? Why or why not?

2. How can you encourage a child or youth who isn't succeeding in a particular sport?

C. Go online to watch a video in which a journalist interviews a parenting expert about children and organized sports. Then check your comprehension.

prod *(n.)* an effort to make someone do something he or she may not want to do

temper tantrum *(n.)* a sudden burst of anger, especially in a child

turn off *(phr. v.)* find something uninteresting

D. Think about the unit video, Listening 1, and Listening 2 as you discuss the questions.

1. What do you think young athletes in both China and the United States are learning from their involvement in competitive sports?

2. In some children's sports leagues, no one keeps score during games, and all the players receive a trophy or medal. The focus is on just having fun. Do you think this is a good idea? Why or why not?

Vocabulary Skill | Idioms

An **idiom** is a particular group of words that has a specific meaning different from the individual words in it. Idioms function as a separate unit, almost as if they were a single word.

To *make a point of* doing something means "to do something because you think it's important or necessary."

☐ The coach **made a point of** congratulating all the players on the winning team.

In a nutshell means "in summary."

☐ Sports can lead to injury, lower grades, and even tension in the family. **In a nutshell**, we must be very cautious when involving our kids in sports.

Because idioms have specific meanings, much like individual words do, it is useful to remember these "chunks" of language in the same way you memorize individual words.

There are thousands of idioms. Most of these idioms are not in the dictionary. For this reason, it is important that you notice them when they occur and use context clues to figure out their meaning.

Tip for Success

Idioms can be difficult to understand in a conversation. If someone uses an idiom that you are not familiar with, use a clarification strategy to ask him or her the meaning of the words.

A. Listen to the excerpts from Listening 1 and Listening 2. Then match each underlined idiom with its definition.

a. left or quit	d. with and in front of other countries
b. pay for something	e. unexpectedly
c. defeated or overcame	

_____ 1. First, I think we've all seen how the Chinese athletes have come <u>out of nowhere</u> in the last twenty years or so and have started to dominate in a number of sports.

_____ 2. In the United States, young athletes and their families have to <u>foot the bill</u>. Sometimes, if they're very good, the athletes can get funding from other sources, such as companies or individuals that want to invest in their athletic careers.

_____ 3. They are proud of their athletes and want their athletes to represent the country <u>on the world stage</u>.

_____ 4. But sometime in the middle of the last century, educators <u>bowed out</u>, and the parents took over, sometimes as coaches, but most often as very active spectators.

_____ 5. And their ambitions often <u>got the best of</u> them.

B. Write sentences using the five idioms in Activity A. Practice saying the sentences with a partner.

1. _____

   _____

Tip for Success

Idioms are a type of collocation. Besides using context, another way to learn the meaning of an idiom is to use a collocations dictionary.

2. _____

   _____

3. _____

   _____

4. _____

   _____

5. _____

   _____

iQ ONLINE **C. Go online for more practice with idioms.**

SPEAKING

At the end of this unit, you are going to share your opinions about good sportsmanship. As you speak, you will need to add to other speakers' comments.

Grammar   Uses of real conditionals

Real conditional sentences show a possible or expected cause and effect. Real conditional statements can give information about the present or the future.

Most real conditionals have a conditional clause containing *if* and a simple present verb connected to a main clause with a simple present or future verb.

conditional clause   main clause

If I **practice** every day, I **will improve** my skills.
(I will improve my skills only by practicing.)

Conditional clauses can also begin with *when* or *whenever* to describe a general truth or habit.

conditional clause   main clause

When I **practice** in the afternoon, I **take** my soccer ball to school with me.
(I only take my soccer ball to school on the days I practice in the afternoon.)

The conditional clause can come before or after the main clause. If the conditional clause comes first, there is a pause, shown by a comma, between the clauses.

I will put on my uniform when I get there.
When I get there, I will put on my uniform.

Real conditionals can be used to express many kinds of ideas.

Things that will become true

☐ If Brazil's team wins tonight, they will be in first place.

Predictions

☐ If we arrive early, we'll probably find a good parking space.

Habits

☐ I prefer to sit in the front row when I go to a game.

Deals, compromises, and promises

☐ If you can drive me to the game, I'll buy the tickets.

Advice

☐ When you throw the ball, remember to lean forward a bit.

Warnings

☐ You will not play in our next game if you show up late to practice.

Instructions

☐ When I pick you up from practice, remember to bring your equipment with you.

A. Read the sentences. Rewrite each one so that the conditional clause comes first. Then practice saying the sentences with a partner.

1. We can continue the game when the rain stops.

   _____

2. I can give you my tickets if you want to go to the game.

   _____

3. You should stay home if you're too sick to go to practice.

   _____

4. I don't like the noise of cheering when I have a headache.

   _____

5. I'll put on my uniform when we get to the baseball field.

   _____

6. We'll play again next week if the game is canceled.

   _____

7. You can't play if you don't show up to the team meeting.

   _____

8. My team wins if you miss this shot.

   _____

stopping a game due to rain

B. Write a conditional sentence for each situation. Then compare answers with a partner.

1. A team member keeps missing practice sessions. He might miss the next one, too. After that, you are going to suspend him from the team.

   Warning: _____

2. A friend is late for his baseball game. You can drive him there. In return, you would like him to buy gas for your car.

   Deal: _____

3. The next game is very important to your team. Winning the game will earn you all a prize.

   Prediction: _____

4. Your friend has trouble hitting a baseball. You notice he needs to hold the bat correctly. That might fix his problem.

   Advice: _____

 C. Go online for more practice with uses of real conditionals.

D. Go online for the grammar expansion.

Pronunciation | **Thought groups**

Speakers don't talk in a steady, continuous stream of words. Instead, they say their words as **thought groups** to help listeners understand their ideas. Speakers separate thought groups with brief pauses.

A thought group may be a short sentence.

| Blake loves basketball. |
| thought group |

It may be part of a longer sentence.

| He plays every day | and watches every game. |
| thought group1 | thought group 2 |

| Steve and Debbie, | on the other hand, | will not be going. |
| thought group 1 | thought group 2 | thought group 3 |

It may be a short phrase or clause.

| Do you agree | or not? |
| thought group 1 | thought group 2 |

The end of a sentence is always the end of a thought group.

| We're going out. | Do you want to come with us? |
| thought group 1 | thought group 2 |

When speaking, think about how to form your ideas into thought groups to help your listeners understand your ideas.

A. Listen to the sentences. Draw slashes (/) between the thought groups.

1. In my opinion,/that's a bad idea.

2. Are they coming or not?

3. If I get home early, I'll go running. Want to join me?

4. Keep your head up as you kick the ball. It's important.

5. All week long these kids are so busy they have no time for fun.

6. If he wins this match, Mr. Williams will be in first place.

7. If you'd like to talk, call me at (555) 233-1157.

8. Here's my email address: goalkeeper100@global.us.

B. Practice reading the sentences in Activity A with a partner. Focus on separating thought groups.

 C. Go online for more practice with thought groups.

| Speaking Skill | Adding to another speaker's comments |

One way to keep a conversation interesting is **to build on someone else's ideas**. Sometimes you want to communicate that you agree with another speaker or add other ideas related to the topic.

These phrases can be used to add to the conversation.

To show agreement	To build on an idea
I agree.	Plus . . .
That's a good point.	Furthermore . . .
That's true.	I would also add (that) . . .
Right.	Another important point is (that) . . .
Exactly.	To build on what you just said . . .
	Going back to what you said before . . .

Phrases of agreement can be combined with phrases that build on an idea.

I agree. I would also add (that) . . .
Exactly. I would also add (that) . . .

Listen to the conversation.

Sung-ju: I believe that organized sports are beneficial to kids. Sports are good exercise, and they give kids the chance to meet people they would never meet otherwise.

David: <u>That's true. And I would add that</u> sports help them learn to work as part of a team.

A. Listen to a discussion about payment for college athletes. Check (✓) the phrases of agreement and the building phrases you hear. Then work with a partner to summarize the main points.

☐ Another important point is that . . .
☐ And to build on what John said earlier, . . .
☐ And I would add that . . .
☐ That's a good point.
☐ Furthermore . . .
☐ Going back to what John said . . .

B. List at least four reasons why you think athletes should NOT be paid while they are in college.

1. _____

   _____

2. _____

   _____

3. _____

   _____

4. _____

   _____

C. Work in a group. Discuss the reasons you listed in Activity B. Agree with or add to the ideas you hear.

iQ ONLINE **D.** Go online for more practice with adding to another speaker's comments.

UNIT OBJECTIVE ▶▶▶▶

In this assignment, you are going to share your opinions about good sportsmanship—the way people behave while participating in sports. As you prepare to share your opinions, think about the Unit Question, "Is athletic competition good for children?" Use information from Listening 1, Listening 2, the unit video, and your work in this unit to support your opinions. Refer to the Self-Assessment checklist on page 202.

CONSIDER THE IDEAS

Work with a partner. Discuss the questions about good sportsmanship.

1. How do team sports help children build social skills?

2. What do winning and losing teach children about life?

3. Does pressure from parents or coaches help children succeed? Why or why not?

4. What personality traits do children gain from sports participation?

5. How involved should parents be in their children's sports activities?

PREPARE AND SPEAK

A. GATHER IDEAS According to the American Academy of Child & Adolescent Psychiatry (AACAP), parents need to get involved in their children's sports and help their children develop good sportsmanship. In a group, brainstorm some ways that parents can follow this advice. Take notes about what you discuss.

Ways for parents to get involved:

_____

_____

_____

_____

_____

Tip for Success

When participating in a group discussion, write down ideas that you think of while others are speaking. This will help you to remember your ideas when you have an opportunity to take a turn.

Good sportsmanship means:

_____

_____

_____

_____

_____

Ways for parents to encourage good sportsmanship:

_____

_____

_____

_____

B. ORGANIZE IDEAS Look over the results of your group's brainstorming session from Activity A. Choose the four ideas you think are the most important. Complete the chart.

Ways to get involved and to encourage good sportsmanship	Benefits to children
1.	
2.	
3.	
4.	

C. **SPEAK** Follow these steps. Refer to the Self-Assessment checklist below before you begin.

1. Conduct a group discussion on this topic: How and why should we encourage good sportsmanship in children?

2. Take turns expressing your ideas. Try to use conditional sentences to express your ideas. Also try to use some of the phrases you learned to add to other speakers' comments. As you speak, use pauses to separate your thought groups.

 Go online for your alternate Unit Assignment.

CHECK AND REFLECT

A. **CHECK** Think about the Unit Assignment as you complete the Self-Assessment checklist.

SELF-ASSESSMENT		
Yes	**No**	
☐	☐	I was able to speak easily about the topic.
☐	☐	My partner, group, and class understood me.
☐	☐	I used real conditional sentences.
☐	☐	I used vocabulary from the unit.
☐	☐	I added to another speaker's comments.
☐	☐	I spoke in thought groups.

 B. **REFLECT** Go to the Online Discussion Board to discuss these questions.

1. What is something new you learned in this unit?

2. Look back at the Unit Question—Is athletic competition good for children? Is your answer different now than when you started this unit? If yes, how is it different? Why?

TRACK YOUR SUCCESS

Circle the words you have learned in this unit.

Nouns
ambition
apex
beneficiary AWL
burnout
era
funding AWL
intensity AWL
journalist
obsession
spectator

Verbs
collapse AWL
conclude AWL
dominate AWL
escalate
invest AWL
regret

Adjectives
brutal
former
fundamental AWL
integral AWL
modest
reasonable
vulnerable

Adverb
ultimately AWL

Oxford 3000™ words

AWL Academic Word List

Check (✓) the skills you learned. If you need more work on a skill, refer to the page(s) in parentheses.

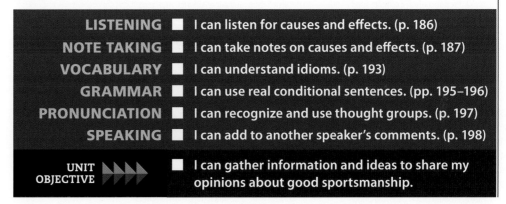

LISTENING	☐ I can listen for causes and effects. (p. 186)
NOTE TAKING	☐ I can take notes on causes and effects. (p. 187)
VOCABULARY	☐ I can understand idioms. (p. 193)
GRAMMAR	☐ I can use real conditional sentences. (pp. 195–196)
PRONUNCIATION	☐ I can recognize and use thought groups. (p. 197)
SPEAKING	☐ I can add to another speaker's comments. (p. 198)
UNIT OBJECTIVE ▶▶▶▶	☐ I can gather information and ideas to share my opinions about good sportsmanship.

AUDIO TRACK LIST

Audio can be found in the *iQ Online* Media Center. Go to **iQOnlinePractice.com**. Click on the Media Center ⬆. Choose to stream or download ⬇ the audio file you select. Not all audio files are available for download.

Page	Track Name: Q2e_04_LS_
3	U01_Q_Classroom.mp3
7	U01_Listening1_ActivityA.mp3
8	U01_Listening1_ActivityD.mp3
12	U01_ListeningSkill_ActivityB.mp3
13	U01_Listening2_ActivityA.mp3
14	U01_Listening2_ActivityC.mp3
18	U01_VocabularySkill_ActivityA.mp3
18	U01_VocabularySkill_ActivityB.mp3
21	U01_Pronunciation_Example1.mp3
21	U01_Pronunciation_Example2.mp3
22	U01_Pronunciation_ActivityA.mp3
22	U01_Pronunciation_ActivityB.mp3
22	U01_SpeakingSkill_ActivityA.mp3
22	U01_SpeakingSkill_ActivityB.mp3
26	U02_Q_Classroom.mp3
29	U02_Listening1_ActivityA.mp3
30	U02_Listening1_ActivityD.mp3
34	U02_ListeningSkill_ActivityA.mp3
35	U02_NoteTakingSkill_ActivityA.mp3
36	U02_Listening2_ActivityA.mp3
37	U02_Listening2_ActivityC.mp3
37	U02_Listening2_ActivityD.mp3
44	U02_Pronunciation_Examples.mp3
44	U02_Pronunciation_ActivityA.mp3
44	U02_Pronunciation_ActivityB.mp3
45	U02_SpeakingSkill_ActivityA.mp3
50	U03_Q_Classroom.mp3
53	U03_NoteTakingSkill_ActivityA.mp3
54	U03_Listening1_ActivityA.mp3
55	U03_Listening1_ActivityC.mp3
59	U03_ListeningSkill_ActivityB.mp3
61	U03_Listening2_ActivityA.mp3
61	U03_Listening2_ActivityC.mp3
68	U03_Grammar_ActivityA.mp3
69	U03_Pronunciation_Example.mp3
69	U03_Pronunciation_ActivityA.mp3
71	U03_SpeakingSkill_ActivityA.mp3
72	U03_UnitAssignment_ActivityA.mp3
77	U04_Q_Classroom.mp3
80	U04_Listening1_ActivityA.mp3
80	U04_Listening1_ActivityC.mp3
83	U04_ListeningSkill_Examples.mp3
84	U04_ListeningSkill_ActivityA.mp3
84	U04_ListeningSkill_ActivityB.mp3
85	U04_NoteTakingSkill_ActivityA.mp3
87	U04_Listening2_ActivityA.mp3
87	U04_Listening2_ActivityD.mp3
95	U04_Pronunciation_ ActivityA.mp3
96	U04_Pronunciation_ ActivityB.mp3
97	U04_SpeakingSkill_ActivityA.mp3

Page	Track Name: Q2e_04_LS_
103	U05_Q_Classroom.mp3
105	U05_NoteTakingSkill_ActivityA.mp3
107	U05_Listening1_ActivityA.mp3
108	U05_Listening1_ActivityD.mp3
110	U05_ListeningSkill_ ActivityA.mp3
110	U05_ListeningSkill_ ActivityB.mp3
112	U05_Listening2_ActivityA.mp3
113	U05_Listening2_ActivityC.mp3
120	U05_Pronunciation_Examples.mp3
120	U05_Pronunciation_ActivityA.mp3
121	U05_SpeakingSkill_ActivityA.mp3
126	U06_Q_Classroom.mp3
129	U06_NoteTakingSkill_ActivityA.mp3
130	U06_Listening1_ActivityA.mp3
131	U06_Listening1_ActivityD.mp3
134	U06_ListeningSkill_ActivityA.mp3
134	U06_ListeningSkill_ActivityB.mp3
135	U06_Listening2_ActivityA.mp3
136	U06_Listening2_ActivityD.mp3
144	U06_Pronunciation_Examples.mp3
144	U06_Pronunciation_ActivityA.mp3
145	U06_Pronunciation_ActivityB.mp3
146	U06_SpeakingSkill_ActivityA.mp3
148	U06_UnitAssignment.mp3
153	U07_Q_Classroom.mp3
155	U07_Listening1_ActivityA.mp3
156	U07_Listening1_ActivityC.mp4
160	U07_ListeningSkill_ActivityA.mp3
161	U07_NoteTakingSkill_ActivityA.mp3
164	U07_Listening2_ActivityA.mp3
164	U07_Listening2_ActivityC.mp3
168	U07_VocabularySkill_ActivityA.mp3
171	U07_Grammar_ActivityA.mp3
172	U07_Pronunciation_Example1.mp3
172	U07_Pronunciation_Example2.mp3
172	U07_Pronunciation_ActivityA.mp3
172	U07_Pronunciation_ActivityB.mp3
173 .	U07_SpeakingSkill_ActivityA.mp3
174	U07_SpeakingSkill_ActivityB.mp3
178	U08_Q_Classroom.mp3
182	U08_Listening1_ActivityA.mp3
183	U08_Listening1_ActivityD.mp3
186	U08_ListeningSkill_ Example1.mp3
186	U08_ListeningSkill_ Example2.mp3
187	U08_ListeningSkill_ActivityA.mp3
188	U08_NoteTakingSkill_ActivityA.mp3
189	U08_Listening2_ActivityA.mp3
191	U08_Listening2_ActivityC.mp3
194	U08_VocabularySkill_ActivityA.mp3
195	U08_Grammar_Examples.mp3

Page	Track Name: Q2e_04_LS_
197	U08_Pronunciation_Examples.mp3
198	U08_Pronunciation_ActivityA.mp3
198	U08_SpeakingSkill_Examples.mp3
199	U08_SpeakingSkill_ActivityA.mp3

AUTHORS AND CONSULTANTS

Authors

Robert Freire holds an M.A. in Applied Linguistics from Montclair State University in New Jersey. He is a teacher and materials developer with more than ten years of ELT experience. He presently teaches ESL and linguistics at Montclair State University.

Tamara Jones holds a Ph.D. in Education from the University of Sheffield in the United Kingdom. She has taught in Russia, Korea, the United Kingdom, the United States, and Belgium. She is currently an instructor at Howard Community College in Maryland. She specializes in the areas of pronunciation and conversation.

Series Consultants

ONLINE INTEGRATION

Chantal Hemmi holds an Ed.D. TEFL and is a Japan-based teacher trainer and curriculum designer. Since leaving her position as Academic Director of the British Council in Tokyo, she has been teaching at the Center for Language Education and Research at Sophia University on an EAP/CLIL program offered for undergraduates. She delivers lectures and teacher trainings throughout Japan, Indonesia, and Malaysia.

COMMUNICATIVE GRAMMAR

Nancy Schoenfeld holds an M.A. in TESOL from Biola University in La Mirada, California, and has been an English language instructor since 2000. She has taught ESL in California and Hawaii, and EFL in Thailand and Kuwait. She has also trained teachers in the United States and Indonesia. Her interests include teaching vocabulary, extensive reading, and student motivation. She is currently an English Language Instructor at Kuwait University.

WRITING

Marguerite Ann Snow holds a Ph.D. in Applied Linguistics from UCLA. She teaches in the TESOL M.A. program in the Charter College of Education at California State University, Los Angeles. She was a Fulbright scholar in Hong Kong and Cyprus. In 2006, she received the President's Distinguished Professor award at Cal State, LA. She has trained EFL teachers in Algeria, Argentina, Brazil, Egypt, Libya, Morocco, Pakistan, Peru, Spain, and Turkey. She is the author/editor of publications in the areas of integrated content, English for academic purposes, and standards for English teaching and learning. She recently served as a co-editor of *Teaching English as a Second or Foreign Language* (4th ed.).

VOCABULARY

Cheryl Boyd Zimmerman is a Professor at California State University, Fullerton. She specializes in second-language vocabulary acquisition, an area in which she is widely published. She teaches graduate courses on second-language acquisition, culture, vocabulary, and the fundamentals of TESOL and is a frequent invited speaker on topics related to vocabulary teaching and learning. She is the author of *Word Knowledge: A Vocabulary Teacher's Handbook* and Series Director of *Inside Reading, Inside Writing,* and *Inside Listening and Speaking,* all published by Oxford University Press.

ASSESSMENT

Lawrence J. Zwier holds an M.A. in TESL from the University of Minnesota. He is currently the Associate Director for Curriculum Development at the English Language Center at Michigan State University in East Lansing. He has taught ESL/EFL in the United States, Saudi Arabia, Malaysia, Japan, and Singapore.

🔑 The keywords of the **Oxford 3000™** have been carefully selected by a group of language experts and experienced teachers as the words which should receive priority in vocabulary study because of their importance and usefulness.

AWL **The Academic Word List** is the most principled and widely accepted list of academic words. Averil Coxhead gathered information from academic materials across the academic disciplines to create this word list.

The Common European Framework of Reference for Languages (CEFR) provides a basic description of what language learners have to do to use language effectively. The system contains 6 reference levels: **A1, A2, B1, B2, C1, C2.** CEFR leveling provided by the Word Family Framework, created by Richard West and published by the British Council. http://www.learnenglish.org.uk/wff/

UNIT 1

acknowledge *(v.)* 🔑 AWL, A2
address *(v.)* 🔑, B2
advance *(v.)* 🔑, B1
aspect *(n.)* 🔑 AWL, A1
assess *(v.)* AWL, A2
capable *(adj.)* 🔑 AWL, B2
contact *(n.)* 🔑 AWL, A1
criticism *(n.)* 🔑, B2
effective *(adj.)* 🔑, A1
ethical *(adj.)* AWL, C1
executive *(n.)* 🔑, A1
exemplify *(v.)*, C2
expert *(n.)* 🔑 AWL, A2
favoritism *(n.)*, C2
issue *(n.)* 🔑 AWL, A1
negotiate *(v.)*, B1
outline *(v.)* 🔑, B1
perspective *(n.)* 🔑 AWL, B1
potential *(n.)* 🔑 AWL, A2
staff *(n.)* 🔑, C1
style *(n.)* 🔑 AWL, B1
title *(n.)* 🔑, A1

UNIT 2

anecdote *(n.)*, C2
appropriate *(adj.)* 🔑 AWL, A1

associate *(v.)* 🔑, C1
bias *(n.)* AWL, B2
cautious *(adj.)*, C1
chaos *(n.)*, B2
conduct *(v.)* 🔑 AWL, A2
cycle *(n.)* 🔑 AWL, B1
embrace *(v.)*, B2
enthusiasm *(n.)* 🔑, B1
inflexible *(adj.)* AWL, B2
investor *(n.)* AWL, B1
moderately *(adv.)*, C2
morale *(n.)*, C1
norm *(n.)* AWL, B2
open-minded *(adj.)*, C1
point out *(phr. v.)*, B2
recognize *(v.)* 🔑, A1
reward *(n.)* 🔑, B2
stifle *(v.)*, C2
stimulating *(adj.)*, B2
stumble upon *(phr. v.)*, C1
trend *(n.)* 🔑 AWL, A2
turn out *(phr. v.)*, A2

UNIT 3

assume *(v.)* 🔑 AWL, A1
barrier *(n.)* 🔑, B1
burden *(n.)*, B1

carefree *(adj.)*, C2
confusion *(n.)* 🔑, B1
contradiction *(n.)* AWL, B2
contribute *(v.)* 🔑 AWL, A2
frustration *(n.)*, B2
guidance *(n.)*, B1
in charge of *(phr.)*, B1
initiation *(n.)* AWL, C2
isolation *(n.)* AWL, B2
marker *(n.)*, C2
milestone *(n.)*, C2
morally *(adv.)* 🔑, C1
pinpoint *(v.)*, C2
resent *(v.)*, C1
reverse *(v.)* 🔑 AWL, B1
run *(v.)* 🔑, A2
satisfaction *(n.)* 🔑, B1
sibling *(n.)*, C1
transition *(n.)* 🔑 AWL, B1

UNIT 4

amateur *(n.)*, C1
appreciation *(n.)* AWL, C1
apprentice *(n.)*, C2
breed *(n.)* 🔑, B2
circulation *(n.)*, B2
clone *(v.)*, C2

convention *(n.)* 🔑 AWL, C2

development *(n.)* 🔑, B2

encounter *(n.)* 🔑 AWL, B1

expand *(v.)* 🔑 AWL, A2

gallery *(n.)*, B1

generation *(n.)* 🔑 AWL, C1

identify with *(phr.)* 🔑, B2

marketing *(n.)* 🔑, B1

operation *(n.)* 🔑, A2

overseas *(adv.)* 🔑 AWL, C1

panel *(n.)* 🔑 AWL, B2

recall *(v.)* 🔑, A2

regard *(v.)* 🔑, A2

series *(n.)* 🔑 AWL, A1

take note of *(phr.)*, C1

unique *(adj.)* 🔑 AWL, A2

UNIT 5

adverse *(adj.)*, C1

alter *(v.)* 🔑 AWL, B1

artificial *(adj.)* 🔑, B2

commodity *(n.)* AWL, B2

compound *(v.)* AWL, C2

consist of *(phr. v.)* 🔑, A2

consume *(v.)* AWL, B1

consumer *(n.)* 🔑 AWL, A1

controversy *(n.)* AWL, B1

debate *(n.)* 🔑 AWL, A1

disturbing *(adj.)* 🔑, C1

ethics *(n.)* AWL, C1

hurdle *(n.)*, C2

identical *(adj.)* AWL, B2

modification *(n.)* AWL, B2

optimal *(adj.)*, C1

reaction *(n.)* 🔑 AWL, B1

significant *(adj.)* 🔑 AWL, A1

substantial *(adj.)* 🔑, A2

superfluous *(adj.)*, C2

trait *(n.)*, C1

ultimate *(adj.)* 🔑 AWL, B1

UNIT 6

advancement *(n.)*, C2

attitude *(n.)* 🔑 AWL, A1

career path *(n.)*, C1

climb the ladder *(phr.)*, C2

commute *(n.)* , C2

concept *(n.)* 🔑 AWL, A1

count on *(phr. v.)* , B2

currently *(adv.)* 🔑, A2

dare *(v.)* 🔑, B1

devote *(v.)* 🔑 AWL, B1

face *(v.)* 🔑, C1

figure *(v.)* 🔑, B1

log *(v.)*, C1

loyal *(adj.)* 🔑, C1

model *(n.)* 🔑, A2

particular *(adj.)* 🔑, A1

peer *(n.)*, B1

point *(n.)* 🔑, A1

radically *(adv.)*, C2

rigorous *(adj.)*, C2

serve one well *(phr.)*, C2

stable *(adj.)* 🔑 AWL, B1

stand out *(phr. v.)*, B2

structure *(n.)* 🔑 AWL, A1

UNIT 7

ache *(v.)*, B1

adhesive *(n.)*, C2

adopt *(v.)* 🔑, A2

alert *(adj.)*, C1

biological *(adj.)*, B1

deprived *(adj.)*, C1

exploit *(v.)* AWL, B1

face to face *(phr.)*, B1

flammable *(adj.)*, C1

in all probability *(phr.)*, C2

inadvertent *(adj.)*, C2

inconceivable *(adj.)* AWL, C2

interact *(v.)* AWL, B2

mandatory *(adj.)*, C1

obvious *(adj.)* 🔑 AWL, A2

odds *(n.)* AWL, B2

reunion *(n.)*, C1

synthetic *(adj.)*, C2

unreliable *(adj.)* AWL, C2

vastly *(adv.)*, C2

UNIT 8

ambition *(n.)* 🔑, B1

apex *(n.)*, C2

beneficiary *(n.)* AWL, C2

brutal *(adj.)*, C2

burnout *(n.)*, B2

collapse *(v.)* 🔑 AWL, B1

conclude *(v.)* 🔑 AWL, A2

dominate *(v.)* 🔑 AWL, B1

era *(n.)* 🔑, B1

escalate *(v.)*, C2

former *(adj.)* 🔑, A1

fundamental *(adj.)* 🔑 AWL, A2

funding *(n.)* AWL, B1

integral *(adj.)* AWL, C1

intensity *(n.)* AWL, B2

invest *(v.)* 🔑 AWL, B1

journalist *(n.)* 🔑, B1

modest *(adj.)*, B1

obsession *(n.)*, C2

reasonable *(adj.)* 🔑, A2

regret *(v.)* 🔑, B1

spectator *(n.)*, C1

ultimately *(adv.)* 🔑 AWL, B1

vulnerable *(adj.)*, B1

OXFORD
UNIVERSITY PRESS

198 Madison Avenue
New York, NY 10016 USA

Great Clarendon Street, Oxford, OX2 6DP, United Kingdom

Oxford University Press is a department of the University of Oxford.
It furthers the University's objective of excellence in research, scholarship,
and education by publishing worldwide. Oxford is a registered trade
mark of Oxford University Press in the UK and in certain other countries

Adult Content Director: Stephanie Karras
Publisher: Sharon Sargent
Managing Editor: Mariel DeKranis
Development Editor: Eric Zuarino
Head of Digital, Design, and Production: Bridget O'Lavin
Executive Art and Design Manager: Maj-Britt Hagsted
Design Project Manager: Debbie Lofaso
Content Production Manager: Julie Armstrong
Image Manager: Trisha Masterson
Image Editor: Liaht Ziskind
Production Coordinator: Brad Tucker

ISBN: 978 0 19 482077 6 Student Book 4B with iQ Online pack
ISBN: 978 0 19 482078 3 Student Book 4B as pack component
ISBN: 978 0 19 481802 5 iQ Online student website

Printed in China
This book is printed on paper from certified and well-managed sources.

ACKNOWLEDGEMENTS

*The authors and publisher are grateful to those who have given permission to
reproduce the following extracts and adaptations of copyright material:*
p. 7 from "The Best of Both Worlds?" by Tara Weiss, *Forbes,* May 23, 2007,
© 2007 Forbes LLC, www.forbes.com. All rights reserved. Used by permission
and protected by the Copyright Laws of the United States. The printing,
copying, redistribution, or retransmission of this Content without express
written permission is prohibited; p. 13 "Myths of Effective Leadership,"
from Center for Creative Leadership *Leading Effectively* Podcast, www.ccl.
org. Used by permission of Center for Creative Leadership; p. 111 "The
'Flavr Savr' Tomato Genetically Modified Food: A Growing Debate #2,"
The World at Six, July 4, 1994, http://www.cbc.ca. Copyright © Canadian
Broadcasting Corporation. All rights reserved. Used by permission of the
Canadian Broadcasting Corporation; p. 106 from "Food additives may cause
hyperactivity: study" by Maggie Fox, Reuters, September 5, 2007, © 2007
reuters.com. All rights reserved. Used by permission and protected by the
Copyright Laws of the United States. The printing, copying, redistribution
or retransmission of this Content without express written permission is
prohibited; p. 135 "'Gap Year' Before College Slowly Catches On With U.S.
Students" from CBS *The Early Show,* June 2, 2003, http://www.cbsnews.com.
Used by permission of CBS News Archives; p. 155 "The Power of Serendipity"
from CBS *Sunday Morning,* Oct. 7, 2007, http://www.cbsnews.com. Used by
permission of CBS News Archives; p. "Against All Odds, Twin Girls Reunited"
from CBS *The Early Show,* April 12, 2006, http://www.cbsnews.com. Used by
permission of CBS News Archives.

Illustrations by: p. 4 Bill Smith Group; p. 52 Claudia Carlson; p. 71 Joe Taylor;
p. 78 Bill Smith Group; p. 104 Barb Bastian; p. 128 Bill Smith Group;
p. 148 Barb Bastian; p. 180 Bill Smith Group.

*We would also like to thank the following for permission to reproduce the following
photographs:* Cover: David Pu'u/Corbis; Video Vocabulary (used throughout
the book): Oleksiy Mark/Shutterstock; p. 2 John Bohn/The Boston Globe via
Getty Images; p. 3 Ascent Xmedia/Getty Images, Trueffelpix/Shutterstock;
p. 4 Goodluz/Shutterstock (Hikers), MBI/Alamy (Meeting); p. 7 Diane Collins
and Jordan Hollender/Getty Images; p. 11 OJO Images Ltd/Alamy; p. 14 Digital
Vision/Oxford University Press; p. 20 Hugh Sitton/Corbis UK Ltd.; p. 27 Rex
Features via AP Images- Google Amsterdam. Photography: Alan Jensen,
Interior Design: D/DOCK; p. 28 White/Oxford University Press (Businessman),
Edward Frazer/Corbis UK Ltd. (Woman), Jetta Productions/Getty Images
(Mechanic); p. 29 Patti McConville/Alamy; p. 35 Cultura RM/Les and Dave
Jacobs/Getty Images; p. 36 michaeljung/Shutterstock (Woman), JGI/Tom
Grill/Getty Images (Man); p. 37 Antenna/Getty Images; p. 43 Image Source/
Oxford University Press (Casual), Stockbyte/Oxford University Press
(Formal); p. 47 paul ridsdale/Alamy; p. 51 epa european pressphoto agency
b.v./Alamy; p. 52 focal point/Shutterstock (Cap), Rebecca Photography/
Shutterstock (Cake), Cheryl A. Meyer/Shutterstock (House); p. 53 Chris
Willson/Alamy (Seijin no Hi), Blend Images/Alamy (Quinceanera); p. 60 Digital
Vision/Oxford University Press (Businessmen), Imagestate Media Partners
Limited - Impact Photos/Alamy (Boys); p. 62 Odua Images/Shutterstock;
p. 76 Atlantide Phototravel/Corbis; p. 77 Peter M. Fisher/Corbis, Happy
person/Shutterstock, dreamtimestudio/Getty Images; p. 78 Larry Lilac/
Alamy (Origami), Gallo Images/Alamy (Jewelry), Deyan Georgiev/Alamy (Bird
house); p. 79 mehmetcan/Shutterstock (Quilt); p. 78 H. Mark Weidman
Photography/Alamy (Group); p. 79 Blend Images/Alamy (Woman); p. 85 Agencja
Fotograficzna Caro/Alamy; p. 86 Kamira/Shutterstock (Tools), Mark Turner/
Getty Images (Cabin); p. 92 Dinodia Photos/Alamy; p. 94 HLPhoto/Fotolia;
p. 99 Ekkapon Sriharun/Alamy (Bag), Roberto Herrett/Alamy (Mannequin),
Juan David Ferrando/Shutterstock (Train), Marius Dragne/Alamy (Cup);
p. 102 All Canada Photos/Alamy; p. 103 Keren Su/Corbis, moodboard/Corbis
(2); p. 105 Bon Appetit/Alamy (Duck), Phanie/Alamy (Oil); p. 106 Dusan Zidar/
Shutterstock (Cereal), Image Source/Oxford University Press (Scientist),
ERproductions Ltd/Getty Images (Woman); p. 111 Jerry Horbert/Shutterstock;
p. 115 Topic Photo Agency IN/Age Fotostock (Canned), Cris Kelly/Alamy
(Canned), Valentyn Volkov/Alamy (Fresh); p. 123 Mira/Alamy (Fresh
raspberries), Farming Today/Alamy (Mouldy raspberries), Food and Drink/
Superstock Ltd. (Chicken outdoors), Michael Blann/Getty Images (Chicken
in lab); p. 127 DIZ München GmbH/Alamy; p. 128 Classic Rock Magazine/
Getty Images (Violinist), pirita/Shutterstock (Vet); p. 130 Photodisc/Getty
Images; p. 135 Neil Setchfield/Alamy; p. 141 EDHAR/Shutterstock;
p. 145 blickwinkel/Alamy (Cheetahs), Hero Images/Getty Images (Campers);
p. 152 TCI/EyeOn/UIG via Getty Images; p. 153 Science Photo Library/Alamy,
Chris Hackett/Tetra Images/Corbis; p. 154 Jim Barber/Shutterstock (X-ray),
bitt24/Shutterstock (Chips), Darkened Studio/Alamy (Dynamite), Cordelia
Molloy/Science Photo Library (Penicillin), GK Hart/Vicky Hart/Getty Images
(Microwave), Inga Nielsen/Shutterstock (Plastic); p. 155 Michael Rosenfeld/
Maximilian S/Superstock Ltd.; p. 157 Donald Erickson/Getty Images
(Cookies), Rob Walls/Alamy (Batteries), Food and drinks/Alamy (Tea),
Purestock/Alamy (Pacemaker), Stuwdamdorp/Alamy (Velcro), jennyt/
Shutterstock (GPS); p. 160 David J. Green - technology/Alamy; p. 161 Guy
Grenier/Masterfile Royalty Free; p. 162 2010 ImageForum/Getty Images
(Lascaux cave paintings), Jean-Daniel Sudres/Hemis/Corb/Corbis UK Ltd.
(Lascaux deer paintings); p. 163 Masterfile Royalty Free; p. 169 Linka A
Odom/Getty Images; p. 174 age fotostock/Superstock Ltd.; p. 179 Bob
Thomas/Getty Images; p. 180 Elvele Images Ltd/Alamy (Running), Michael
Ventura/Alamy (Tae Kwon Do), Russell Sadur/Getty Images (Soccer);
p. 181 2012 AFP/Getty Images; p. 188 Blend Images/Alamy; p. 189 PCN
Photography/Alamy; p. 190 Steve Skjold/Alamy; p. 196 Will Iredale/
Shutterstock; p. 200 Pressmaster/Shutterstock (Tennis), Eliza Snow/Getty
Images (Fencers).